Painless Borders

Sally Schneider

That Patchwork Place®

Dear Georgine!
May all your quilts
be painless!
Sally Schneider
Nov. 1993

CREDITS

Photography . . . . Doug Plager
Illustration and Graphics . . . . Laurel Strand
Cover Design . . . . Judy Petry
Text Design . . . . Shea Dutton
Editor . . . . Barbara Weiland
Copy Editor . . . . Jane Meyer

Painless Borders ©
© 1992 by Sally Schneider
That Patchwork Place, Inc.,
PO Box 118, Bothell, WA 98041-0118

Printed in the United States of America
97 96 95 94 93 92   6 5 4 3 2 1

Library of Congress Cataloging-in-Publication Data

Schneider, Sally.
   Painless borders / Sally Schneider.
      p. cm.
      ISBN 0-943574-98-6
      1. Patchwork—Patterns. 2. Borders, Ornamental
      (Decorative arts)
   I. Title
   TT835.S3469 1992   92-1306
   746.9'7—dc20   CIP

Published in the USA

ACKNOWLEDGMENTS

Many thanks go to the following people who helped in so many ways:

Margy Fisher, whose tulip quilt started the whole idea of Painless Borders.

Barb Eikmeier, for her continued encouragement, thoughtful criticism, and unflagging support.

Sue Linker, Judy Sogn, Cheri Potts, and Nancy Koorenny, for proofreading and helping to clarify directions.

The friends who made quilts: Eileen Sherrill, Maureen McGee, Barb Eikmeier, Cheri Potts, Nancy Koorenny, Iva Galloway, Doris Morelock, Nancy Nogues.

The friends who quilted quilts: Pat Cole, Joan Henderson, Ellen Koehn, Lois Boulware, Maureen McGee.

The friends who tested the patterns: Betty Flannigan, Carroll Kellogg, Cathy Barnes, Pam Montgomery, Sara Calderwood, Ida Heger, Jerry Creed, Grace Jackson.

Nancyanne Twelker for permission to use her Pine Tree block design.

Judy Martin for permission to use Piecemaker's Block and Peace on Earth from her book *Scraps, Blocks & Quilts* by Judy Martin, ©1990.

Dick, for his way with words, and especially his patience.

And for Ted, who likes every quilt I make.

TABLE OF CONTENTS

PREFACE

In 1983 a friend sent me a photograph of a quilt she had made using a pieced tulip block. The blocks were set on the diagonal and there were Ninepatch blocks around the outside edge. These Ninepatch blocks were colored so that they formed what appeared to be a border around the quilt which I found very attractive.

The idea of the Ninepatch block border simmered in my mind until the spring of 1990, when I needed to make some sample quilts for a class I was teaching. I used the Ninepatch border in one of the quilts, but in the other I changed some of the units in the border block to checkerboard squares. I thought it looked more interesting that way. The idea of changing some of the units of the border block led me to my favorite question: "What if?"

The ability to design on a computer let me see the answer very quickly, but it led to more questions: What if I use triangles? What if I piece the edge triangles? What if I color this a little differently?

It was like eating peanuts; I couldn't stop. I designed page after page of wonderful, complex borders, and still there were more. Books were full of pictures of quilts with pieced borders as were all the quilt magazines, and I tried to draft each border I saw into a block unit. Some of them were more successful than others. The most successful ones are presented in this book. As for the concept, I thank Mary Ellen Hopkins, whose pattern for the tulip quilt was the inspiration for Painless Borders.

INTRODUCTION

"I really want to put a pieced border on this quilt. I'm tired of just adding strips around the outside, but it's so hard to figure out how to make a pieced one. I'm not sure where to begin."

How many times have you said or thought those words? How often have you heard friends or members of your quilt guild express that frustration?

Pieced borders can be an exquisite finishing touch on a quilt, a beautiful frame for your picture. On many quilts they are quite necessary to complete the desired image. But complex pieced borders can also be an overwhelming construction challenge, so much so that many of us seldom attempt to make them or we avoid them altogether.

Many of the most successful pieced borders seem to have their main elements set on the diagonal. Drafting the pattern for them requires the maker to calculate the diagonal measurements of the units using decimals and then to convert the result to inches. This method leaves much room for error between the calculator and the quilt. It is very easy to end up with too much or too little border, making it necessary to stretch or ease the pieces somewhere, or even to add extra fabric to the quilt to make the border fit. This can alter the look you desire, and occasionally it can spoil the quilt entirely. Making pieced borders with elements set on the diagonal is a challenging undertaking.

A quilt with its blocks set on the diagonal isn't as great a challenge to construct. With a slight shift of the imagination, you may see that it is possible to translate many of those diagonal border elements into block designs. Then, by setting the blocks of the quilt on the diagonal and using block designs on the outside edge of the quilt which are different from those in the major design area, and by limiting the components of all the blocks to those which can be quick-pieced, you can create an easily constructed, dynamically designed, intricately bordered work of art. Piecing the border as blocks rather than as a separate part of the quilt eliminates the need for complicated math formulas. It also eliminates the frustration of "fudging" borders to make them fit.

The quick-pieced designs in this book are based on series of squares. Some of these squares are subdivided into other shapes, but the main design is divided like a grid. The most commonly used grids are the Ninepatch,

the sixteen-square Four Patch, and the twenty-five-square Five Patch. These grids are shown below.

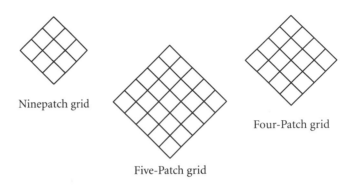

Ninepatch grid

Four-Patch grid

Five-Patch grid

Painless Borders are based on these same grids. The diagrams below show how, by using a contrasting color, you can subdivide a Ninepatch block to give the illusion of a border. In the first diagram, the Ninepatch blocks around the outside edge of the quilt are pieced with dark squares diagonally through the block. The remaining squares are light. Examine the diagram to see the effect of the border of squares on the diagonal.

By adding half-square triangle units on each side of the dark squares, the border is changed to one very commonly seen on pieced quilts. I call it the squares and triangles border.

Replacing some of the squares with checkerboards changes the design, giving the quilt yet another look.

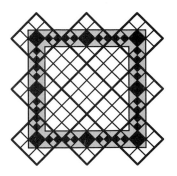

This is the basic theory of *Painless Borders*. Blocks are set on the diagonal and different design elements are used for the blocks around the edge of the quilt.

In this book I have included nine pieced border designs. Most of them are designs I have seen on quilts in shows or in books or magazines. Each border has been adapted to fit three different grids: a Ninepatch grid, a sixteen-square, Four-Patch grid, and a twenty-five square, Five-Patch grid.

I chose these grids because they seem to be the ones most commonly used. As I examined diagrams for quick-pieced blocks, I found that the books showed many blocks in those categories, but fewer in the larger grid categories.

The border designs are shown colored in dark and light to show several different versions for each border. The designs can change by altering the placement of the dark and light fabrics, emphasizing different parts of the border design. They are also shown in the appendix along with the outlines of the blocks required to make them, so you can experiment with your own dark/light combinations or color ideas.

The quilt designs are almost unlimited, because they change with the block designs you choose in the center. Making one of these quilts allows you to pick a block of your choice and frame it with any of the nine borders, selecting the style that best suits your block design and your grid size.

Block designs are not limited to piecing. Some of the examples show appliqué blocks bordered with pieced blocks of the same size. For example, a 12" finished appliqué block could be bordered with a Ninepatch border block if each square of the border block measured 4", or it could be bordered with a sixteen-square Four-Patch border block if each square of the border block measured 3".

The gallery of quilts on pages 18–30 shows at least two versions of each border design, each one made on a different grid base.

Specific directions are included for each of the borders; they are contained within the instructions for the quilt with that border. General directions for piecing each of the block designs, as well as patterns for the appliqué designs, are included. Two of the block designs require templates, but most pieced blocks are constructed using quick-piecing techniques. The appliqué designs are stitched by machine using the blind hem stitch and invisible nylon thread.

Wall Quilts

When designing wall-sized quilts using the Painless Borders technique, you may find that there is not enough space separating the blocks and border, but expanding the space between them by adding plain squares causes the central design to appear too isolated.

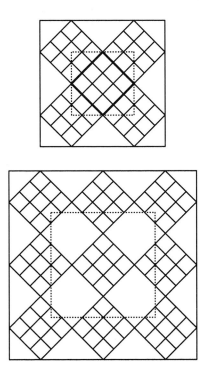

One solution to the problem is to use as the center design a block which contains more grid squares than the border block. To do this in a wall quilt, which uses only one design block, you may borrow space from adjacent plain squares for the center design.

Ninepatch grid

The diagrams at left show each of the three most commonly used grids with the center square outlined by darker lines. The larger square around the center square is created by borrowing one row of the grid from each adjacent square. Use all the area inside the larger dark square, as outlined in the diagram, to achieve a more dominant central design in a wall hanging. By sketching the design on the schematic, you will see that it is just as easy to construct these quilts in blocks which are slightly different from traditional block designs.

16-Square, Four-Patch Grid

The Bear's Paw block drawn in the center of a twenty-five square Five Patch grid illustrates this technique. The quilt made using this design is on page 22. Try some of your favorite blocks on the Four-Patch and Five-Patch grids.

Another device to fill a large empty space is to replace the plain squares with snowball blocks. The quilt on page 22 shows snowball blocks used with the Bear's Paw block; these snowball blocks were constructed with only two contrasting corners, rather than the usual four. The blocks are made by using the "folded corner" technique; the corners are twice the size of a single square of the grid. See page 11.

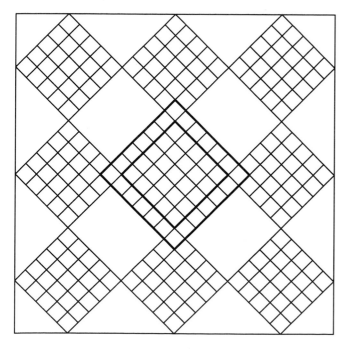

25-Square, Five-Patch Grid

FABRIC CHOICES

While most fabric designs are appropriate for Painless Borders quilts, there are some special circumstances which deserve consideration.

The fabric used on the outside edge will be cut into several pieces, rather than being one continuous strip. Therefore, it's best to avoid stripes, directional prints, widely-scattered large prints, and solids that show the interruption in the fabric design.

By contrast, densely designed prints and large florals disguise seam lines, making them excellent candidates for *Painless Borders*.

The background fabric requires the same consideration; it might also be cut into several pieces between the design area and the beginning of the border. Prints—small and unobtrusive, large and overall, muted-color and tone-on-tone—tend to disguise the seams, while all the seam lines tend to show in solid-colored fabrics.

In the actual design area of the quilt, most fabric designs are appropriate, including medium-to-large prints, geometric designs, plaids, small scattered prints, and solids. Variety in the size and style of prints gives a quilt a look of excitement and motion that doesn't occur when only prints of similar size and style are used. Combining small, unobtrusive prints with larger, multicolored prints creates an interesting design, while also providing a comfortable visual resting place. It is the combination of all these factors—color, design and texture—which makes a quilt a stimulating visual experience.

Examples of appropriate and inappropriate fabric choices. The group at the bottom make good Painless Borders, while the group at the top are not good choices.

CONSTRUCTION TECHNIQUES

SEAM ALLOWANCES

All seam allowances are ¼" wide. Unfortunately, the distance from the needle to the right edge of the presser foot is not always ¼", and not all ¼" measurements on rulers are the same. This can lead to inaccuracies in sewing. The solution is twofold. First, always use the same ruler, and be sure that it is accurate. Second, mark the bed of your sewing machine with the ¼" measurement from your ruler, and follow this mark when sewing quilt pieces together.

To mark your sewing machine, place the ruler on your sewing machine. With the presser foot in the up position, align the ¼" ruler line with the sewing machine needle. Lower the needle slowly until it touches the ¼" line. Lower the presser foot to help keep the ruler in position. Align the ruler with another mark or line somewhere on the sewing machine to be sure that the line you will draw is straight. Using a permanent marker with a fine point, draw a line along the edge of the ruler. This will be your ¼"-wide seam allowance guide line.

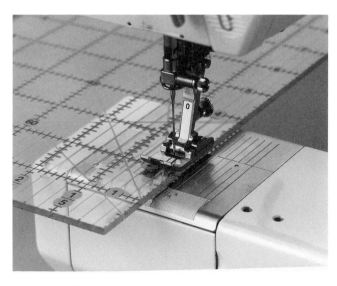

Mark the throat plate of your sewing machine with the same ¼" that is on your ruler.

Test the seam allowance by cutting three 2"-wide strips of scrap fabric of 100% cotton, similar to the fabric you will be using in your quilt. They should be about 6" long. Stitch the three strips together using the ¼" seam allowance guide line you marked on the machine. Press the seams to one side, pressing the pieced set flat. Measure the width; it should be *exactly* 5". If it is not, adjust the line until it is correct (the marks come off with alcohol if you need to remove

them). Keep adjusting the line and testing it until you can sew the correct seam allowance.

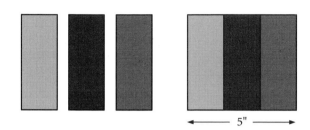

The line should stay on your machine permanently so that you can always refer to it, but when you are sewing pieces together, it is helpful to have more than just a line to guide your fabric. A ridge is much more useful. Many people use several layers of masking tape, or a piece of "moleskin" padding, available at drug stores. A magnetic seam guide attachment is a helpful alternative if one is available for your machine. Whatever method you use to mark the seam allowance, the drawn line should be your first reference. Then, if for some reason you have to remove the tape, you can replace it without having to measure the seam allowance again.

The drawn line is your first reference. Keep the material you use to mark your seam allowance away from the feed dogs.

Whatever material you use to form this ridge, be careful not to let it get under the presser foot, as this would prevent feeding the fabric at an even pressure. The fabric does not feed straight under the needle if the presser foot is impeded.

TOOLS AND CUTTING

Quick piecing requires specialized tools: a rotary cutter, a cutting mat, and an acrylic ruler. My favorite ruler is 6" x 24" and has both a horizontal and vertical grid marked in ⅛" increments.

To cut with the rotary cutter, push it through the fabric along the edge of the ruler using a smooth motion and consistent pressure. If the blade does not cut all layers, press a little harder. With a little experience, it will become apparent how much pressure to use and how many layers of fabric you can cut through with ease.

Before cutting strips it is essential to straighten the edge of your fabric. Begin by folding the ironed fabric in half, matching the selvages.

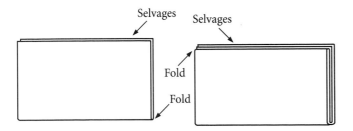

Fold the fabric again, lining up the fold of the fabric with the selvages. You now have four layers of fabric.

Using your ruler, line up one of its horizontal lines with the folded edge of the fabric (opposite the side with the selvages). Slide the ruler toward the raw edge on the left side of the fabric until it is as close to the edge as possible with all four layers of fabric underneath.

Cut along the edge of the ruler, trimming off the uneven edge of fabric. Discard the trimmings. Now that the edges are all straight, you can begin cutting strips by using the vertical measuring lines of the ruler. Measure the size strips you want by lining up the vertical line which determines your required size with the cut edge of the fabric.

STRIP PIECING

Blocks or parts of blocks made with just squares and rectangles can be assembled quickly by cutting strips of fabric a specific width, sewing them together in a particular order called a set, then cutting the sets apart and combining them with other sets of pieces made the same way.

Sew strips together in the order required for your design—this is called a set. Press with a hot steam iron, but press carefully to avoid stretching the fabric. Press set from the right side. Although the sets may tend to curl, they must be pressed straight. After pressing the right side, turn the set over and press from the wrong side, being sure that all seam allowances are pressed flat and to one side. Press seams toward the darker fabric.

Now you are ready to cut across these sets at specified intervals to form rows or blocks for your quilt. Trim the edge of the set using the seam lines as the horizontal guide for your ruler. The selvage of the fabric is removed in this step.

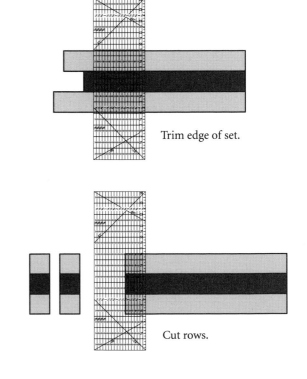

Trim edge of set.

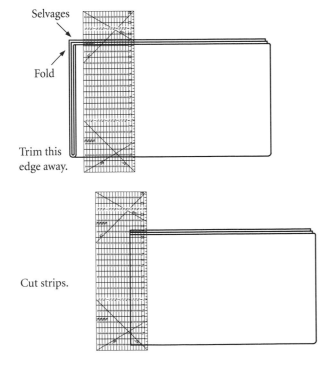

Trim this edge away.

Cut strips.

Cut rows.

Cut rows from the set using the width specified in your directions. You can usually cut two or three sets of strips at one time, but any more tend to slip out of position and the resulting pieces are inaccurate.

To sew rows together, match the intersecting seam lines with seam allowances lying in opposite directions. Pin intersections on either side of the actual seam, through the seam allowances.

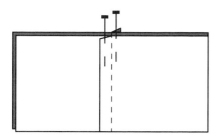

Pin intersections

When matching points of triangles, keep the point you must match on top so that you can see it. You will be able to see an intersection of seams on the wrong side of the squares. It looks like a Y.

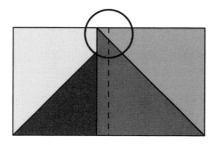

Be sure to sew right through the intersection of the seams so that the point is not cut off by the stitching.

If you must match a point to a point, as in eight-point centers, push a pin directly through both points and pull it snug. Place a pin on each side of the first pin, through the seam allowances, and remove the first pin. Stitch through the intersection of the seams.

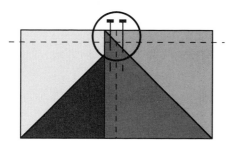

Press seams as you sew them. Press them to the darker side whenever possible; otherwise, press seams so that opposing seam allowances are facing opposite directions. When pressing, avoid stretching or otherwise distorting bias edges.

FOLDED CORNERS

Occasionally in patchwork designs there are rectangles or large squares whose corners are made from triangles of another fabric, as shown in the examples below. It is a simple matter to construct these units using only squares rather than triangles, without being concerned with the correct diagonal measurements and seam allowances. This method results in a little more fabric waste, but the time and energy saved are well worth it.

1. Determine the size of strips needed to form the basic design unit by adding ½" for seam allowances to the required finished size of the square. For example, if the design is based on a 2" finished square, cut folded corner pieces 2½" square.
2. Cut squares the determined size.
3. On the wrong side of the square, mark the diagonal with a pencil or pen.
4. Cut the underlying piece (either a rectangle or a larger square). Remember to add seam allowances to the desired finished size.
5. Lay the contrasting square on top of the base piece, right sides together, checking to see that the diagonal line points in the proper direction.

6. Stitch on the diagonal line.
7. Trim away the excess fabric.

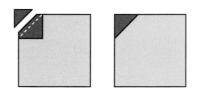

8. Press the remaining triangle to the corner of the square or rectangle.
9. Repeat for remaining corners if required.

These folded corners are frequently used to subdivide plain squares placed between pieced blocks, or on the tip of edge triangles where they provide a continuous straight line for the edge of the border.

QUICK-PIECED TRIANGLES

Half-Square Triangle Units

To quickly produce a large quantity of squares consisting of two right-angle triangles, the grid system described below is fast and accurate. This method requires two pieces of fabric placed right sides together, a ruler with a grid marked in ⅛" increments and a very sharp pencil or other marking implement. Mechanical pencils and black fine-point pens work well for marking, as do silver, white or yellow pencils if you keep their points sharp.

I prefer to draw grids on the lighter of the two fabrics and cut the grid out after it is drawn. Leave about ½" of space all around the grid when cutting it out to provide working room.

For ease in sewing and for the sake of accuracy, the grid should be no larger than three squares by four squares, for a total of 12 squares.

All directions in this book are based on preparing full grids with 12 squares or half grids with six squares, unless otherwise noted. A full grid will yield 24 half-square triangle units. A half grid will yield 12 units.

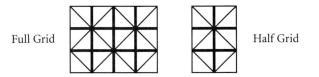

Full Grid   Half Grid

The size of the squares for the grid is determined by adding ⅞" to the required finished size of your triangle square. This demands that you sew an accurate ¼"-wide seam allowance on all sides of the triangle. If the distance from the needle to the edge of your presser foot is not exactly ¼", you can make a marking guide to compensate for that. (See Marking Guides on page 13.) Using either the ⅞" measurement or your marking guide, draw a grid of squares on the back of the lightest fabric. Begin by drawing a horizontal line on your fabric close to the edge, then measure the required distance and draw another line. Repeat to the end of your fabric.

Line up a horizontal line on your ruler with one of the lines you have drawn to determine an exact 90° angle. With the ruler near the edge of the fabric, draw a vertical line. Measure the required distance and draw another line. Repeat to the end of your fabric. Your fabric will resemble the squares of a checkerboard.

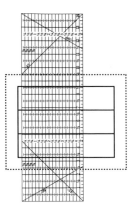

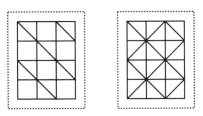

Now draw diagonal lines through all the squares, alternating the direction of the drawn lines so you can sew along them without ever cutting your thread.

Draw a diagonal line in every other row of squares in one direction, then in every other row of squares in the other direction.

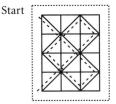

Check the grid; you should have one diagonal line in each square. *If a square has an* X *through it, it is incorrect and you must redraw the lines.*

To help keep the two pieces of fabric from slipping, press them together before you begin sewing, or pin them together.

Examine the diagonal lines carefully and you will see that you can trace a continuous line through the whole grid without ever lifting your pencil. That means you can also sew a continuous line through the grid without ever cutting your thread.

Begin sewing in a corner. Place the edge of your presser foot on the drawn line and sew a straight line to the end of the line. With the needle in the down position, rotate the fabric 90°, then continue sewing to the next corner. Rotate again and sew. Keep rotating 90° and sewing straight lines until you reach the end (the corner opposite from where you started stitching).

Start   Finish

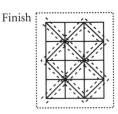

Grid half sewn   Grid completely sewn

Now rotate the fabric 180° and stitch ¼" away from the opposite side of the grid lines, ending in the same corner where you started stitching the first half of the grid. When you are finished, you should have a line of stitching on each side of each diagonal line.

Cut the grid apart exactly on each drawn line. For each square of the grid that you drew, you will have two half-square triangle units.

Press the seams to one side or the other. Directions for the specific quilt you are making often tell you which way to press. If not, it is usually safe to press toward the darker half of the unit.

You will also find little triangles sticking out beyond the square on two corners after you have pressed the seam allowances. Trim off to reduce bulk.

Quarter-Square Triangle Units

Quick-pieced half-square triangles can also be used as the basis for quarter-square triangles. For all these units, the squares in the grid should be 1¼" larger than the desired finished size of the square. If the distance from the needle to the edge of your presser foot is not exactly ¼" wide, see "Marking Guides" below.

Place two half-square triangle units, with either identical or different fabrics, right sides together, matching seam lines. Draw a diagonal line that crosses the seam line. With the presser foot on the line as a guide, sew on each side of the diagonal line. Cut on the drawn line and you will have the two units shown below.

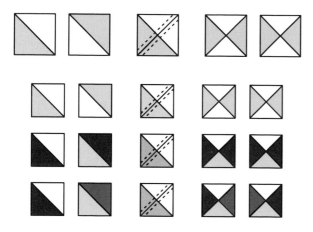

Some designs in this book require another similar unit which is made of one half-square triangle and two quarter-square triangles. To make these, begin with half-square triangle units constructed on a grid which is 1¼" larger than the required finished size (or use your marking guide). These units should be made with the two fabrics which will be the quarter-square triangles.

Using the fabric for the half-square triangle, cut a square ⅞" larger than the required finished size (or the same size as the half-square triangle unit). With these pieces right sides together, draw a line diagonally through the square, crossing the seam of the half-square triangle unit. Stitch ¼" on each side of the line. Cut on the line and you will have the units shown below. Careful control of fabrics is required to achieve the desired shape and color arrangement.

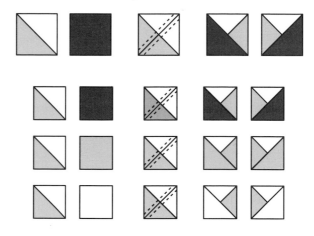

MARKING GUIDES

Because the measurement from the needle to the outside edge of the presser foot is not always exactly ¼" wide, corrections must be made for this variation when marking grids for Quick-Pieced Triangles. You can either purchase a foot which meets this criterion, if one is available for your machine, or you can make marking guides which take this difference into account. To make them you will need heavy template plastic or heavy poster board. These marking guides will be used to draw the checkerboard of squares only, not for drawing diagonal lines or cutting.

Begin by drawing a square of the required finished size on a sheet of paper. Do not use graph paper. Use the ruler you normally use to cut strips. Be sure the square is as precise as you can possibly make it.

Draw a diagonal line through the square, extending the line for about 1" at each end.

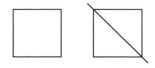

Remove the thread from your sewing machine and place the right edge of the presser foot on this diagonal line. Stitch a line parallel to the drawn line on the paper.

Sew on the left side of the line.

With your ruler, add ¼"-wide seam allowances to the two adjacent sides of the square opposite the sewn diagonal line. Extend these seam allowances to the sewn line.

Measure from the top of the square to the intersection of the sewn line and the ¼" seam allowance line. Use this measurement to make a marking guide for quick-pieced triangles of this size on your machine. (See below.)

Make your marking guide this size.

You will need a different marking guide for each size half-square triangle unit you want to make.

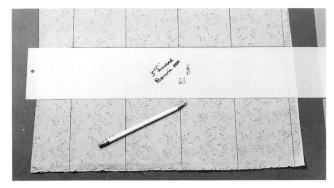

Use this guide to create the grid on the layered fabric.

This method will also work for quarter-square triangles. Draw a square of the required finished size as you did above, but this time draw diagonal lines both ways through the square. Add the ¼" seam allowance on the top of the square.

With the edge of the presser foot on the diagonal line, sew parallel to both diagonal lines and measure the distance between the intersections of the sewn lines and the ¼" seam allowance line to determine the size of your marking guide.

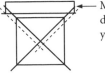

Measure here to determine the size of your marking guide.

To make the marking guide, measure the required distance as calculated above and mark this measurement on template plastic. Place acrylic ruler on the plastic, making sure all vertical lines are parallel, and score the plastic lightly with an old rotary cutter blade. Then bend the plastic until it snaps on the scored line.

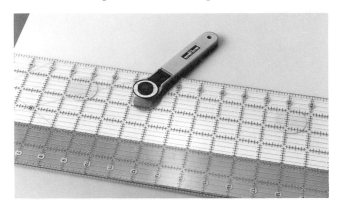

To make the marking guides, measure the required distance as calculated above and mark this measurement on the template plastic.

Occasionally the ruler may slip on the template plastic; to prevent this, place small rubber circles or pieces of rubber band between the plastic and the ruler.

After you have made your marking guide, check it to see that it is accurate, and that the measurements on both ends are the same. Use this guide to create the grid on the layered fabric.

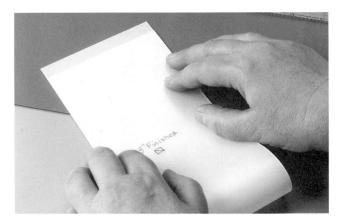

After you have made your marking guide, check it to see that it is accurate, and that the measurements on both ends are the same.

DIAGONAL SETS

Piecing the blocks of a quilt together when they are set on the diagonal is no more difficult than piecing a quilt using a straight set, but there are some tricks to make it easier.

When blocks are set on the diagonal, there are triangular-shaped areas on the edges and at the corners that must be filled, either with pieced triangles (partial blocks), or with plain triangles. In *Painless Borders* quilts, these triangles are occasionally pieced. But whether pieced or plain, the triangles must be constructed with the straight grain of the fabric on the longest edge of the triangle (except for the corner pieces, which will be discussed later). This places the straight of grain rather than the bias on the outside edge of the quilt, making it easier to attach borders or binding without stretching the quilt top.

For plain triangles:

1. Measure the diagonal of your completed block.

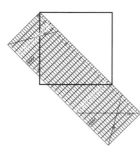

2. Add 2" to that measurement.
3. Use this new measurement to cut squares of the chosen fabric.
4. Cut the squares twice diagonally to yield four triangles.

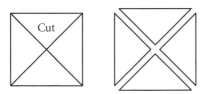

These triangles are much larger than necessary for your quilt, but because sewing places stresses on bias edges, the outside edges tend to curve inward. Therefore, if you cut triangles exactly the right size, they would shrink inward and might end up being too small. It is so easy to trim off the extra, and impossible to add more to it!

Place these edge triangles in the spaces at the edge of your quilt and piece them to the ends of the blocks as you sew the rows together, following the diagram.

Note: See below for cutting corner triangles shown in the illustration.

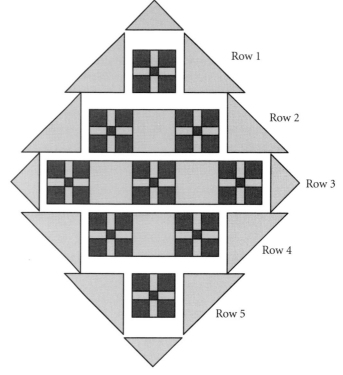

Notice that the right angle points of the triangles are kept on the same line as the block edges, and the sharper points of the triangles are allowed to overhang the block. It is essential to keep that edge straight. When you are sewing one row to another, you can easily stitch over the points that stick up and trim them off after the row has been sewn.

Cut the corners from squares cut the same size as your pieced squares. Then cut these squares in half on the diagonal, to yield two triangles. You will need to cut two of these squares for every quilt to yield four triangles, one for each corner.

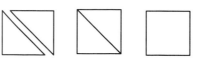

Some *Painless Borders* quilts require pieced edge triangles in order to allow the border design to properly flow around the quilt. These triangles must still be constructed with their outside edge on the straight grain of the fabric.

Those edge-triangle units which require triangles to be pieced on their tips can be constructed using the folded corners technique described on page 11. Cut the square for the folded corner the same size as the cut square for the blocks you are making, or a multiple of that size. If your folded corner represents more than one square of grid, it will be cut the size of the multiple, plus the ½" additional for seam allowances. The examples below show two folded corners. The first example uses a folded corner that represents only one square of the grid. If the grid unit squares finish 2" and are cut 2½", the square for the folded corner is cut 2½".

Folded corner cut the same size as one square of the block unit

In the example below, the folded corner represents two squares of the grid. If the original squares finish 2", the square for this folded corner is cut 4½" square, which is twice the size of the original square plus ½" for seam allowances.

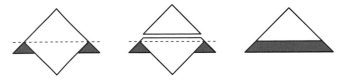

Folded corner cut twice the size as one square of the block unit

In the case of edge triangles which require a complete square at the apex, the easiest way to construct the unit is to cut the large square, which will be cut in quarters diagonally, one inch larger than required. (Rather than cutting a 15" square to make edge triangles to fit blocks with a diagonal measurement of 13", cut the square one inch larger—16".)

Cut a strip from one side of the triangle the same width as the pieced square (including seam allowances). Sew the pieced square to the top of the strip, then reassemble the large triangles and trim off the excess fabric on the bottom of the strip. When cutting the strip from the side of the triangle, be sure to always cut from the same side of the triangle. Otherwise it is very easy to end up with pieced units at the apex of the triangle going in the wrong direction.

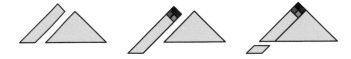

If there are three squares on the apex of the edge triangles as shown in the diagram below, add 2" to the size of the large square which will be cut in quarters diagonally. Cut two strips from the side of the resulting

triangles and add squares as shown. Reassemble the large triangle and trim excess at the bottom edge.

In the example below, only the small outside triangles (the ones colored in gray) are cut with the long edge on the straight grain. To measure the square required to cut these triangles, measure the diagonal of the small square, add 2" to that measurement and cut squares that size from the outside edge fabric. Cut the squares in quarters diagonally.

Once the quilt top is completed, check to see that opposite sides of the quilt are equal. Carefully fold it in half lengthwise, matching seam intersections on opposite sides. If the sides are not the same length, resew the diagonal seams which join rows together on the longer side, taking a slightly deeper seam. Just an extra ⅛" in each row will add up to a 1" adjustment for every four rows that are restitched.

Repeat this step, folding the quilt in half crosswise, to measure the top and bottom of the quilt.

Until a diagonally set quilt is layered and basted for quilting, it is extremely important to use care when handling it. The vertical and horizontal planes of these quilts are on the bias and will stretch very easily. While basting, be sure to pat the quilt flat rather than to push fullness to one edge. Also, take care that you do not stretch or distort the fold lines when you fold up the unquilted and unbasted top. You may stretch the center of the quilt so much that it will never lie flat.

THE QUILT PLANS

The following section has specific directions for sixteen quilts, all of which are pictured in the quilt gallery. Each border design is represented at least once in these directions. Directions are written for the size quilt that is shown.

All borders take advantage of quick-piecing, Template-free™ techniques, although two of the block designs require the use of templates. These can be found on pages 70–71. All measurements given include a ¼"-wide seam allowance, and all units will fit together if you are consistent.

One of the quilts requires appliqué blocks. The templates and block sketches for these designs are included with the directions for that quilt.

The fabrics required to make each quilt are identified by color, referring to the color photograph of that specific quilt. You may substitute your own color choices for those listed if you wish. It is helpful to make a color reference card for each quilt you are making. On this card, write the color as listed in the directions; next to it, either write your own color choice or attach a small swatch of the chosen fabric.

All fabric requirements have been calculated to allow some extra fabric. As a general rule, yardage requirements under 2 yards include ¼ yard extra, and yardage requirements over 2 yards include ½ yard extra. All fabric requirements depend on fabric that has 40" of usable width after it is washed and the selvages are removed.

When you must cut several different-sized units from strips, always cut the larger pieces first, then cut the smaller pieces from the remainder of the strips.

All directions for half-square triangles in this book are based on preparing full grids with twelve squares or half grids with six squares, unless otherwise noted. A full grid will yield twenty-four half-square triangle units. A half grid will yield twelve units.

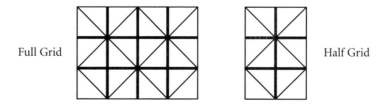

Full Grid   Half Grid

Quilts are graded by difficulty in the following manner:

Easy — appropriate for someone with basic quick-piecing skills. Can probably be constructed in less than 12 hours (depending on how quickly you sew).

Intermediate — somewhat more complex in design, requiring basic quick-piecing skills, but more time—probably 12–20 hours. The wall hangings which borrow space from other blocks, page 6, are all included in this category because more experience is needed to visualize the designs.

Advanced — requires more advanced piecing skills and/or more time to construct.

Stars and Squares, *Sally Schneider, 1990, Puyallup, Washington. 50" x 63". A quilt similar to this was shown in Marsha McCloskey's* Stars and Stepping Stones. *The center design is made from two easy blocks, the Ohio Star and a Ninepatch block with checkerboard corners. The checkerboards are repeated in the border, combined with triangles. To maintain continuity in the border design, some of the Ninepatch blocks have triangles in one or two corners. Red, white and blue is always an effective color combination, particularly with star patterns. The different background fabric used for the border makes it stand out from the quilt background.*

Maple Leaf Rag, *Barbara Eikmeier, 1991, Manhattan, Kansas. 37½" x 50". Named for the Scott Joplin musical composition, Maple Leaf Rag is a good example of the sparkle that a pieced border can add to a simple block.*

Delectable Mountains, *Sally Schneider, 1990, Puyallup Washington. 60" x 60". A long-time favorite pattern, Delectable Mountains is very easy to make using quick-pieced triangles. The low contrast between the large border print and the black triangles heightens the effect of the border.*

Second Time Around, *Nancy Lee Nogues, 1991, Puyallup, Washington. 42" x 56". This quilt featuring the Old Maid's Puzzle block was Nancy's second attempt at the design. When blocks are rotated in alternate rows, they form a large star in the center. Careful choice of fabrics is necessary to make the border stand out.*

Celebration, *Doris P. Morelock, 1991, Alexandria, Virginia. 47" x 47". Doris used a block from Judy Martin's* Scraps, Blocks & Quilts *with a Pinwheel Chain border for her quilt. The happy combination of complex pieced blocks and quick-pieced border blocks of the same size makes this Painless Borders quilt shine. The red fabric in the center star provides just the right zing.*

Stars and Stripes Forever, *Cheri L. Potts, 1991, Puyallup, Washington. 32" x 32". The choice of patriotic fabrics and the Eccentric Star block with a border of triangles makes a wonderful wall hanging. Cheri chose this design to commemorate the momentous events of 1991.*

Bear's Paw, *Sally Schneider, 1991, Puyallup, Washington. 42" x 42". This wall quilt uses the technique of borrowing space from adjacent blocks to complete a design. The plain blocks provide a good area for fancy quilting while the partial Snowball blocks made with folded corners help fill up the space between the blocks and the border, and expand the design.*

***Shining Stars**, Iva Willard Galloway, 1991, Puyallup, Washington. 42" x 52". A beautiful blend of blues and the Ohio Star design makes a very restful quilt. The plain squares provide a place to show off your quilting.*

See Saw, *Sally Schneider, 1991, Puyallup, Washington. 56" x 70". The border print was the inspiration for choosing the fabrics in this quilt. The design was the successful product of a sleepless night. When blocks are set next to each other and arranged on the diagonal, an interesting subordinate design is created. Quilted by Ellen Koehn.*

Shoo Fly, *Sally Schneider, 1991, Puyallup, Washington. 63" x 74". This simple, traditional design has a new impact when set on the diagonal and surrounded with rows of squares. The gold background provides rich contrast with the simplicity of the quilt design. Quilted by Lois Boulware.*

Confetti Medallion, *Sally Schneider, Puyallup, Washington, 1991. 98" x 112". I've always admired medallion quilts with a central focus and several borders, but the thought of calculating sizes for all the pieces kept me from making one. The Painless Borders concept was the solution. Combining several different borders made the calculations a snap. The confetti design was introduced in my first book, Scrap Happy, but its use here as a central medallion demonstrates its versatility. All parts of the quilt are constructed using just half-square triangles and folded corners. The teal accent fabric sets off the reds and blues used for the stars and pinwheels.*

Christmas Ribbons, *Sally Schneider, 1991, Puyallup, Washington. 70" x 84". A bright white background and cheery Christmas fabrics combine with a striking Folded Ribbon border to produce a splendid holiday quilt. Believe it or not, a grocery-store display of gift boxes was the inspiration for this design. The border was inspired by the quilt "Christmas Celebration" by Barbara Dieges, shown on the cover of* Quilting Today, *Issue #22.*

Spring Garden Basket, *Eileen Broyles Sherrill, 1991, Seoul, Korea. 32" x 32". The floral border and pastel points in the Shaded Triangle border beautifully frame a basket block.*

Flowers in a Cut Glass Dish through a Shattered Window, *Eileen Broyles Sherrill, 1991, Seoul, Korea. 32" x 32". Eileen wasn't happy making just one quilt from the basket design! She also wanted to make one with solids, although solids are not recommended for Painless Borders quilts. Her quilt is the exception that breaks the rule, and her exquisite hand quilting provides just the right finishing touch.*

Quiltmaker's Dreams, *Maureen H. McGee, 1991, Lansing, Kansas. 50" x 66". Maureen started with a block from Judy Martin's* Scraps, Blocks & Quilts *and then designed a border of Pinwheels to frame it. Her choice of cloudlike fabric for the background and border gives the whole quilt a dreamlike quality.*

Appliqué Sampler, *Sally Schneider, Puyallup, Washington, and Barbara Eikmeier, Manhattan, Kansas, 1991. 42" x 42". A set of eight appliqué templates were arranged in different ways to create the block designs for this little quilt. A Pleated Ribbon border using blocks that are the same size as the appliqué blocks provides a very effective frame for the designs. Barbara did the appliqué and Sally pieced and quilted the quilt.*

Snow Crystals, *Nancy A. Koorenny, 1991, Puyallup, Washington. 36" x 36". This design borrows space for the center block from the surrounding blocks. The repetition of the Pleated Ribbon effect of the block in the border produces a stunning wall quilt.*

STARS AND SQUARES

Lap Size

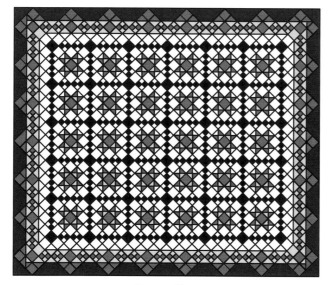

Queen Size

Twin Size

Photo	Page 18			
Skill Level	Advanced			
Border Style	Big and Little Squares and Triangles			
Finished Block Size	9"			
Quilt Size:	Lap Quilt:	50" x 62½"		
	Twin Quilt:	62½" x 87½"		
	Queen Quilt:	87½" x 100"		

Materials: 44"-wide fabric

	Lap	Twin	Queen
☐ **Light**	1¾ yds.	3½ yds.	5¼ yds.
▨ **Blue Floral**	1¾ yds.	2¼ yds.	3⅛ yds.
■ **Red**	¾ yd.	1 yd.	1¾ yds.
▢ **Red Check**	1½ yds.	1¾ yds.	2¾ yds.
■ **Blue Confetti**	1 yd.	1½ yds.	2 yds.

Batting, backing, binding and thread to finish

Cutting

To simplify the construction of this quilt, first cut the number of strips required for your quilt from each of the colors as shown below. When the block directions call for specific square sizes, cut them from the appropriate strips.

	Strip Width	Quilt Size		
		Lap	Twin	Queen
Light	2"	4	8	15
	3½"	7	16	29
Blue Floral	2"	3	4	6
	3½"	4	6	8
Red	2"	4	8	15
	3½"	2	3	4
Red Check	2"	3	4	6
	3½"	2	3	3

Star Blocks

1. Construct the full and half grids for quarter-square triangles shown in the chart below, using a 3" finished size and following the directions on page 13. Cut and press.

	Lap	Twin	Queen
Light/Blue Floral	1 grid	1½ grids	3 grids
Blue Floral/ Red Check	1 grid	1½ grids	3 grids

Lap	Make 12 half-square triangle units.
Twin	Make 30 half-square triangle units.
Queen	Make 60 half-square triangle units.

Lap	Make 14 half-square triangle units.
Twin	Make 32 half-square triangle units.
Queen	Make 62 half-square triangle units.

(Reserve extras for border blocks.)

2. Using 1 half-square triangle unit from each group, construct the required number of quarter-square triangle units as shown.

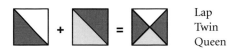

Lap	Make 24.
Twin	Make 60.
Queen	Make 120.

3. Crosscut 3½" squares from the 3½"-wide strips of Light and Blue Floral as indicated:

	Lap	Twin	Queen
Light	24	60	120
Blue Floral	6	15	30

4. Assemble the star blocks as shown, using the quarter-square triangle units and the squares of Light and Blue Floral. Make the required number for the quilt size you are making. Set aside extra half-square triangle units.

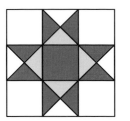

Lap	Make 6.
Twin	Make 15.
Queen	Make 30.

Checkerboard Blocks

1. Sew 2"-wide strips of Light and Red fabrics together in the required number of sets for your quilt size. Cut them into 2"-wide segments and then sew them in pairs to make checkerboards as shown.

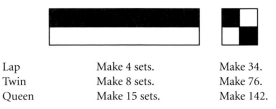

Lap	Make 4 sets.	Make 34.
Twin	Make 8 sets.	Make 76.
Queen	Make 15 sets.	Make 142.

2. Using Light and Red Check fabrics, construct the full and half grids shown in the chart below. Use a 3" finished size and follow the directions for half-square triangle units on page 12. Cut and press.

Lap	Make 34.
Twin	Make 52.
Queen	Make 70.

Lap	**Twin**	**Queen**
1½ grids	2½ grids	3 grids

3. Crosscut 3½" squares from the 3½"-wide strips of Light and Red fabrics as indicated:

	Lap	Twin	Queen
Light	48	96	168
Red	12	24	42

4. Using the checkerboards, half-square triangle units and squares, assemble the three different blocks as shown.

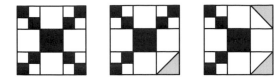

Lap	Make 2.	Make 6.	Make 4.
Twin	Make 8.	Make 12.	Make 4.
Queen	Make 20.	Make 18.	Make 4.

Border Blocks

Two different border blocks are required. Block #1 is used for the sides and Block #2 gracefully turns the border corner.

1. Sew 2"-wide strips of Blue Floral and Red Check fabrics together in the required number of sets for your quilt size. Cut them into 2"-wide strips and then sew them in pairs to make checkerboards as shown.

Lap	Make 3 sets.	Make 28 squares.
Twin	Make 4 sets.	Make 40 squares.
Queen	Make 6 sets.	Make 52 squares.

2. Using Blue Floral and Red Check fabrics, construct the full and half grids shown in the chart below. Use a 3" finished size and follow the directions for half-square triangle units on page 12. Cut and press.

Lap	Make 28.
Twin	Make 40.
Queen	Make 52.

Lap	Twin	Queen
1½ grids	2 grids	2½ grids

3. Crosscut 3½" squares from the 3½"-wide strips of fabrics as indicated:

	Lap	Twin	Queen
Light	10	16	22
Blue Floral	32	44	56
Red Check	4	4	4

4. From Blue Floral, cut 2 squares, 3⅞" x 3⅞". Using 2 half-square triangle units made of Blue Floral and Red Check (left over from Star blocks) and the Blue Floral squares, construct 4 of the units as shown below.

5. Assemble blocks as shown.

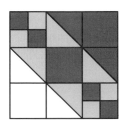

Lap	Make 10.	Make 4.
Twin	Make 16.	Make 4.
Queen	Make 22.	Make 4.

Edge and Corner Triangles

1. From Blue Confetti fabric, cut the required number of 15" squares. Cut twice diagonally to yield the required number of edge triangles.

	No. of Squares	No. of Edge Triangles
Lap	4	14 (2 extra)
Twin	5	20
Queen	7	26 (2 extra)

2. Crosscut 3½" squares from the 3½"-wide strips of Red Check fabric as indicated:

	No. of Squares
Lap	14
Twin	20
Queen	26

3. Sew a 3½" Red Check square to the tip of each edge triangle, following the directions for folded corners on page 11.

4. From the Blue Confetti fabric, cut two 9" squares. Cut once diagonally to yield 4 corner triangles.

Quilt Assembly

1. Arrange blocks and triangles as shown in the quilt plan on page 31.
2. Stitch together into rows; sew rows together.
3. Add batting and backing. Quilt as desired. Bind edges. See Quilt Finishing, page 72.

MAPLE LEAF RAG

Photo	Page 18	
Skill Level	Easy	
Border Style	Big and Little Squares	
Finished Block Size	9"	
Quilt Size	37½" x 50"	

Materials: 44"-wide fabric

⬛ **Leaf Colors**	1 yd. of a single color or equivalent in scraps*	
⬛ **Dark (stems)**	1" x 44" strip	
⬜ **White**	1¼ yds.	
⬛ **Brown**	½ yd.	
⬜ **Gold**	1⅝ yds.	

Backing, batting, binding and thread to finish
* A 9" x 12" scrap is enough for 1 leaf.

Maple Leaf Blocks

1. Using White and a single Leaf Color and a 3" finished grid size, construct 1 full grid and 1 half grid, following the directions for half-square triangles on page 12. Cut and press. OR, make 4 half-square triangle units of each different leaf color desired.

 Make 32.

2. Cut the following 3½" wide strips and crosscut as indicated.

	No. of Strips	Crosscut into:
White	2	16 squares, 3½" x 3½"
Leaf Color	3	24 squares, 3½" x 3½"

Note: If you are making the leaves in different colors, you will need 3 leaf color squares and 2 white squares for each Maple Leaf block.

3. For stems use the 1" x 44" strip of Dark fabric, or use 1" x 5" strips of fabric to match each leaf. Turn under both long edges of the strip and press, forming a finished strip ½" wide. (Use Bias Bars or the Clover Bias Maker if you have them to make this step easier.)

4. Topstitch or hand appliqué the prepared strip diagonally down the center of 8 white squares.

5. Using the half-square triangle units and the 3½" squares, construct the Maple Leaf blocks as shown. Make 8 blocks.

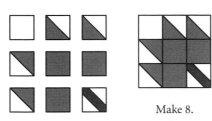

Make 8.

Border Blocks

1. Cut the following strips of fabric.

	Strip Width	No. of Strips
White	2"	1
	3½"	1
Brown	2"	2
	3½"	1
Gold	2"	1
	3½"	1

2. Sew strips together to make strip sets and crosscut into the required segments as shown below.

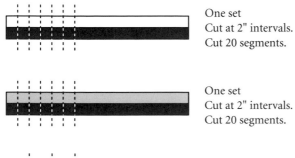

One set
Cut at 2" intervals.
Cut 20 segments.

One set
Cut at 2" intervals.
Cut 20 segments.

One set
Cut at 3½" intervals.
Cut 10 segments.

3. Make 20 checkerboard squares, using the segments cut in step 2.

Make 20.

4. Cut the following 3½"-wide strips and crosscut into squares and rectangles indicated:

	No. of Strips	Crosscut into:
White	2	6 rectangles, 3½" x 6½"
		10 squares, 3½" x 3½"
Gold	4	14 rectangles, 3½" x 6½"
		10 squares, 3½" x 3½"

5. Using the checkerboards, squares and rectangles, construct the blocks as shown.

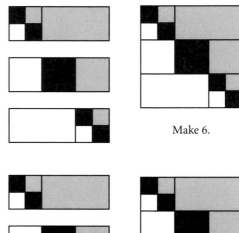

Make 6.

Make 4.

Edge and Corner Triangles

1. From Gold, cut three 15" squares and cut twice diagonally to yield 12 edge triangles. You will use 10 of these.

2. From Gold, cut two 9" squares and cut once diagonally to yield 4 corner triangles.

Quilt Assembly

1. Arrange blocks and triangles as shown in the quilt plan on page 34.

2. Stitch together into rows; sew rows together.

3. Add batting and backing. Quilt as desired. Bind edges. See Quilt Finishing, page 72.

OLD MAID'S PUZZLE

Photo   Page 20
Skill level   Easy
Border Style   Big and Little Squares
Finished Block Size   10"
Quilt Size   42" x 56"

Materials: 44"-wide fabric

- ■ **Red**   ¾ yd.
- ■ **Pink**   1 yd.
- ▨ **Blue**   1¾ yds.
- ☐ **Ecru**   1¾ yds.

  Batting, backing, binding and thread to finish

Design Blocks

1. Using Red and Ecru fabrics and a 2½" finished grid size, construct 2 full grids, following the directions for half-square triangles on page 12. Cut; press seams toward darker half of each unit. Repeat with Pink and Ecru fabrics.

2. Cut the following 3"-wide strips and crosscut as indicated:

	No. of Strips	Crosscut into:
Pink	2	16 squares, 3" x 3"
Ecru	3	32 squares, 3" x 3"

3. Construct 8 blocks as shown.

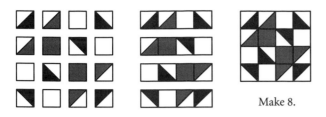

Make 8.

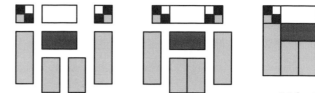

Make 4.

Border Blocks

1. From Red, cut 2 strips, 1¾" wide.
   From Ecru and from Blue, cut 1 strip each, 1¾" wide. Assemble strip sets as shown and crosscut into segments, 1¾" wide.

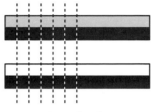

Make 1 of each set.

Make 20 checkerboard units as shown.

Make 20.

2. Cut the following 3"-wide strips and crosscut as indicated:

	No. of Strips	Crosscut into:
Pink	2	12 squares, 3" x 3"
		4 rectangles, 3" x 5½"
Blue	6	6 squares, 3" x 3"
		14 rectangles, 3" x 5½"
		14 rectangles, 3" x 8"
Ecru	4	6 squares, 3" x 3"
		10 rectangles, 3" x 5½"
		6 rectangles, 3" x 8"

3. Construct the border and corner blocks as shown, being careful to position the checkerboard pieces correctly.

  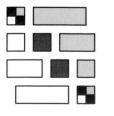

Make 6.

Edge and Corner Triangles

1. Cut three 16" squares from Blue. Cut twice diagonally to yield a total of 12 edge triangles. You will use 10 of these.
2. Cut two 10" squares from Blue. Cut once diagonally to yield a total of 4 corner triangles.

Quilt Assembly

1. Arrange blocks and triangles as shown in the quilt plan on page 36.
2. Stitch together into rows; sew the rows together.
3. Add batting and backing. Quilt as desired. Bind edges. See Quilt Finishing, page 72.

DELECTABLE MOUNTAINS

Photo	Page 19
Skill Level	Intermediate
Border Style	Squares and Triangles
Finished Block Size	8"
Quilt Size	60" x 60"

Materials: 44"-wide fabric

☐	**Ecru**	2¾ yds.
■	**Black Print**	2½ yds.
▨	**Pink**	1¼ yds.
■	**Black**	1¼ yds.
▨	**Green**	⅜ yd.

Batting, backing, binding and thread to finish

Three different blocks are required. Two of them require the same pieces with only slight color variations. The third block forms the border.

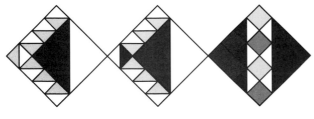

Block 1   Block 2   Border Block

Block #1

1. Using Pink and Ecru fabrics and a 2" finished grid size, construct 4 grids, following the directions for half-square triangles on page 12. Cut and press.

 Make 84.

2. Using the Black Print and Ecru fabrics and a 6" finished grid size, construct 1 half grid for half-square triangles. Cut and press.

 Make 12.

3. Assemble the units shown below.

Make 12.   Make 12.

4. Make 12 blocks, following piecing diagram below.

Make 12.

Block #2

1. Using the Pink and Ecru fabrics and a 2" finished grid size, construct 3 grids for half-square triangles. Cut and press.

 Make 12.

2. Using the Black and Ecru fabrics and a 2" finished grid size, construct 1 half grid. Cut and press.

 Make 12.

3. Using the Black Print and Ecru fabrics and a 6" finished grid size, construct 1 half grid for half-square triangles. Cut and press.

 Make 12.

4. Assemble the units shown below.

 Make 12.

Make 12.

5. Make 12 blocks, following the piecing diagram below.

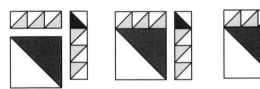

Make 12.

Border Blocks

1. Using the Black and Ecru fabrics and a 2" finished grid size, construct 4 full grids and 1 half grid. Cut and press.

 Make 100.

2. Cut the following strips and crosscut into the squares and rectangles indicated:

	Strip Width	No. of Strips	Crosscut into:
Ecru	2½"	1	16 squares, 2½"x 2½"
Black Print	2½"	3	16 squares, 2½"x 2½"
			16 rectangles, 2½"x 4½"
Pink	2½"	2	32 squares, 2½" x 2½"
Black	4½"	2	16 squares, 4½" x 4½"
Green	2½"	2	32 squares, 2½" x 2½"

3. Sew one 2½" Ecru square to one corner of each 4½" Black square, following the directions for folded corners on page 11.

4. Make 16 blocks, following the piecing diagram below.

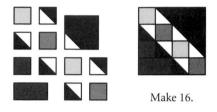

Make 16.

Pieced Edge Triangles

1. From Black Print, cut five 15" squares. Cut each square twice diagonally to yield 20 triangles.
2. Cut a 2½"-wide strip from one side of each triangle. Using the reserved half-square triangle units, stitch one unit to the straight end of each strip, making sure the triangle unit is positioned correctly.

3. Reassemble the edge triangles and trim as shown.

Quilt Assembly

1. Arrange blocks and triangles as shown in the quilt plan on page 38.
2. Stitch together into rows; sew rows together.
3. Add batting and backing. Quilt as desired. Bind edges. See Quilt Finishing, page 72.

SHOO FLY

Photo   Page 25
Skill Level   Intermediate
Border Style   Multiple Squares
Finished Block Size   Lap Quilt: 6"
                      Comforter: 7½"
                      Twin Quilt: 9"
Quilt Size   Lap Quilt: 52" x 60"
                      Comforter: 63" x 73½"
                      Twin Quilt: 75" x 87"

Materials: 44"-wide fabric

	Lap	**Comforter**	**Twin**
■ **Blue**	¾ yds.	1 yd.	1⅛ yd.
■ **Paisley**	1 yd.	1¾ yds.	2 yds.
■ **Red**	¾ yd.	1⅛ yds.	1¼ yds.
☐ **Gold**	3¼ yds.	5¼ yds.	6¼ yds.

Batting, backing, binding and thread to finish

Shoo Fly Blocks

1. Using the Paisley and Gold fabrics, construct 4 full grids, following the directions for half-square triangles on page 12. Be sure to use the correct finished grid size for the quilt size you are making (2" finished for Lap, 2½" finished for Comforter and 3" finished for Twin quilt). Cut and press. Each quilt requires 80 half-square triangle units. (You will have some left over.)   Make 80.

2. Cut the following strips from the Blue and from the Gold fabrics and then sew the strips together in Blue/Gold pairs.

	Strip Width	**No. of Strips**
Lap	1½"	5 of each color
Comforter	1¾"	7 of each color
Twin	2"	8 of each color

3. From the strip pairs, crosscut 80 squares, cutting them 2½" square for the lap quilt, 3" square for the comforter, or 3½" square for the twin quilt.

4. From Red, cut the following strips, crosscutting them into squares as indicated:

	Strip Width	No. of Strips	Crosscut into:
Lap	2½"	2	20 squares, 2½" x 2½"
Comforter	3"	2	20 squares, 3" x 3"
Twin	3½"	2	20 squares, 3½" x 3½"

5. Assemble 20 Shoo Fly Blocks as shown.

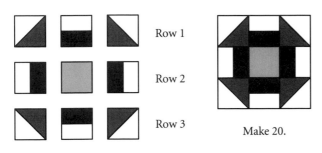

Row 1

Row 2

Row 3

Make 20.

Border Blocks

This quilt requires 18 border blocks and 4 corner blocks. The plain squares surrounding the border on the inside all have 1 pieced corner, and the plain squares on the corner have 2 pieced corners.

1. Cut the following strips from fabrics indicated:

	Strip Width	Blue	Paisley	Red	Gold
Lap	1½"	5	10	10	5
Comforter	1¾"	6	12	12	6
Twin	2"	7	14	14	7

2. Sew strips together as shown.

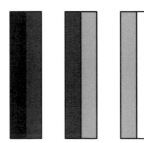

Lap	Make 5 sets of each.
Comforter	Make 6 sets of each.
Twin	Make 7 sets of each.

3. Crosscut each strip set into segments the same width as you cut the individual strips for your quilt size. You should have 124 segments of each color combination. In addition, cut 4 squares from each strip set to use when constructing the corner blocks in step 7 below. Cut the squares 2½" square for the lap-size quilt, 3" square for the comforter, and 3½" square for the twin-size quilt.

 Make 4 of each.

4. Using the segments cut in step 3 above, construct checkerboard squares as shown.

 Make 62.   Make 124.

5. Cut the following strips from Gold fabric and crosscut into squares as indicated:

	Strip Width	No. of Strips	Crosscut into:
Lap	2½"	3	44 squares, 2½" x 2½"
Comforter	3"	4	44 squares, 3" x 3"
Twin	3½"	4	44 squares, 3½" x 3½"

6. Using checkerboard squares and Gold squares, make 18 border blocks as shown.

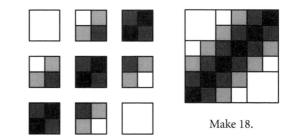

Make 18.

7. Using checkerboard squares, Gold squares, and strip-set squares reserved in step 3, make 4 corner blocks as shown.

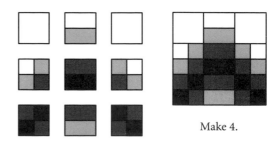

Make 4.

Reserve the remaining checkerboard squares for the Alternating Squares and Edge Triangles, on page 42.

Alternating Squares

The Shoo Fly blocks are set together with alternating plain squares, but the ones around the edges of the quilt have checkerboards in one or two corners.

1. Cut the following strips from Gold, crosscutting them into the segments indicated:

	Strip Width	No. of Strips	Crosscut into:
Lap	6½"	5	* 14 squares, 6½" x 6½"
			18 rectangles, 4½" x 6½"
Comforter	8"	6	* 14 squares, 8" x 8"
			18 rectangles, 5½" x 8"
Twin	9½"	7	* 14 squares, 9½" x 9½"
			18 rectangles, 6½" x 9½"

* Reserve 2 squares for the corner triangles.

2. Cut the following strips from Gold and crosscut into segments indicated:

	Strip Width	No. of Strips	Crosscut into:
Lap	2½"	2	18 rectangles, 2½" x 4½"
			4 squares, 2½" x 2½"
Comforter	3"	3	18 rectangles, 3" x 5½"
			4 squares, 3" x 3"
Twin	3½"	3	18 rectangles, 3½" x 6½"
			4 squares, 3½" x 3½"

3. Using the pieces cut in steps 1 and 2 above, and 22 of the reserved checkerboard squares, assemble the alternating blocks as shown.

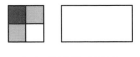

Make 14.

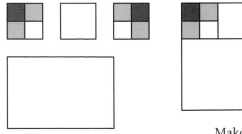

Make 4.

Edge and Corner Triangles

1. From Gold, cut 6 squares, making them 12" square for the lap quilt, 14" square for the comforter and 16" square for the twin quilt. Cut squares twice diagonally to yield a total of 24 triangles. You will use 22.

2. Cut a strip from one side of each of 22 edge triangles.

	Strip Width
Lap	2½"
Comforter	3"
Twin	3½"

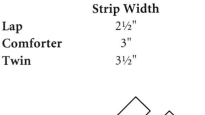

3. Stitch a reserved checkerboard to the straight end of each strip, then reassemble each edge triangle and trim as shown.

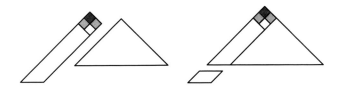

4. Cut the 2 Gold squares (reserved earlier) in half diagonally to yield 4 corner triangles.

Quilt Assembly

1. Arrange blocks and triangles as shown in the quilt plan on page 40.
2. Stitch together into rows; sew the rows together.
3. Add batting and backing. Quilt as desired. Bind edges. See Quilt Finishing, page 72.

CHRISTMAS RIBBONS

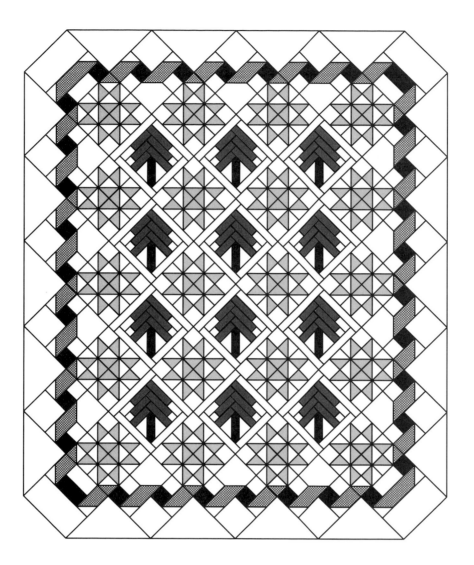

Photo	Page 27	
Skill Level	Advanced	
Border Style	Folded Ribbon	
Finished Block Size	Lap Quilt: 8"	
	Twin Quilt: 10"	
Quilt Size:	Lap Quilt: 56" x 67"	
	Twin Quilt: 70" x 84"	

Materials: 44"-wide fabric

	Lap Quilt	Twin Quilt
☐ **White**	4⅞ yds.	7 yds.
☐ **Assorted Reds** (stars)	1¾ yds. total	2 yds. total
☐ **Assorted Reds and**		
Greens (branches)	¾ yd. total	⅞ yd. total
☐ **Brown** (tree trunks)	⅛ yd.	⅛ yd.
☐ **Red** (ribbon)	1 yd.	1¼ yds.
☐ **Green** (ribbon)	⅜ yd.	½ yd.

Tree Blocks

1. Cut the following strips and crosscut into squares and rectangles as indicated:

Lap Quilt	Strip Width	No. of Strips	Crosscut into:
Assorted Reds	1½"	12	(no crosscuts)
and Greens (branches)			
Brown	1"	2	
White	1½"	12	24 squares, 1½" x 1½"
			24 rectangles, 1½" x 2½"
	3½"	2	12 squares, 3½" x 3½"

Twin Quilt	Strip Width	No. of Strips	Crosscut into:
Assorted Reds and Greens (branches)	1¾"	12	(no crosscuts)
Brown	1"	2	
White	1¾"	17	24 squares, 1¾" x 1¾"
			24 rectangles, 1¾" x 1¾"
	4¼"	2	12 squares, 4¼" x 4¼"

2. Fold under ¼" on each long edge of the tree trunk strips and press, forming a ½"-wide finished strip. Place the strip on a large White square for the tree base and stitch by hand or machine along one edge, adding the remaining squares, chain fashion, as you stitch, until you reach the end of the strip. Stitch the remaining side of the strip. Repeat with remaining strip and squares. Cut apart.

3. Place 1 tree strip, right sides together, with a completed base square. Stitch. Trim strip even with edge of square. Repeat on the adjacent side of the base square.

4. Sew a White square to each end of the next tree strip.

Add another pair of strips (branches) to the block, placing the white squares at opposite corners of the block as shown.

5. Sew a White rectangle to each end of the next tree strip and add a third pair of strips to the block.

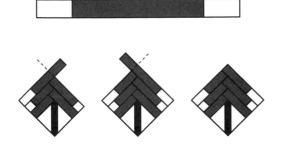

6. Sew a strip of background fabric to all 4 sides of the tree block.

Make a total of 12 trees following steps 3 through 6.

Star Blocks

This quilt requires the three different star blocks shown below. The difference is in the corners. The stars were pieced from an assortment of colors, but you may wish to use only one or two colors.

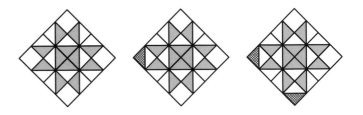

1. Using White and assorted Reds for stars and the appropriate finished grid size for the quilt you are making (2" finished for Lap and 2½" finished for Twin), construct 12 full grids for half-square triangles. Follow the directions on page 12. Cut and press. (If using only 1 or 2 fabrics, make only 10 grids.)

   Make 240.

2. Using White and Red (for ribbon) and the correct finished grid size (step 1, above), construct 1 full grid for half-square triangles. Cut and press.

   Make 18.

3. Cut the following strips of White and crosscut into squares indicated:

	Strip Width	No. of Strips	Crosscut into:
Lap Quilt	2½"	4	62 squares, 2½" x 2½"
Twin Quilt	3"	5	62 Squares, 3" x 3"

4. Using half-square triangle units and White squares, assemble the Star blocks as shown.

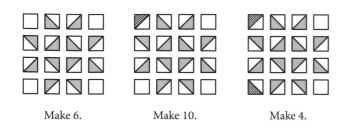

Make 6.   Make 10.   Make 4.

Border Blocks

This quilt requires the 4 different border blocks shown below. You will use two of them for the corner squares (two each), one of them for the top and bottom, and the remaining one for the sides.

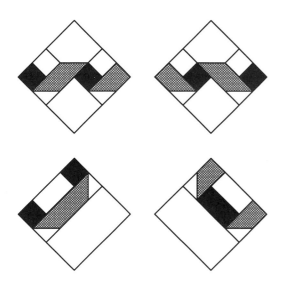

1. Using White and Red (for ribbon) and the correct finished grid size for the quilt you are making (2" finished for Lap and 2½" finished for Twin), construct 1 full grid and 1 half grid for half-square triangles. Cut and press.

2. Cut the following strips and crosscut into squares and rectangles as indicated:

Lap Quilt	Strip Width	No. of Strips	Crosscut into:
White	4½"	5	28 squares, 4½" x 4½"
			4 rectangles, 4½" x 8½"
			4 rectangles, 2½" x 4½"
	2½"	2	32 squares, 2½" x 2½"
Red (ribbon)	2½"	4	46 squares, 2½" x 2½"
			2 rectangles, 2½" x 8½"
Green (ribbon)	2½"	3	32 squares, 2½" x 2½"
			2 rectangles, 2½" x 4½"

Twin Quilt	Strip Width	No. of Strips	Crosscut into:
White	5½"	6	28 squares, 5½" x 5½"
			4 rectangles, 5½" x 10½"
			4 rectangles, 3" x 5½"
	3"	3	32 squares, 3" x 3"
Red (ribbon)	3"	6	46 squares, 3" x 3"
			2 rectangles, 3" x 10½"
Green (ribbon)	3"	3	32 squares, 3" x 3"
			2 rectangles, 3" x 5½"

3. Sew a Red square to each of 14 large White squares, following the directions for folded corners on page 11. Sew White squares to both ends of Red rectangles in the same manner.

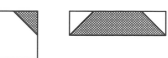

5. Assemble border blocks, using squares, rectangles and half-square triangle units as shown.

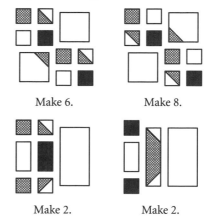

Make 6.   Make 8.

Make 2.   Make 2.

Edge Triangles and Corner Rectangles

1. For lap quilt, cut five 13½" White squares. For twin quilt, cut five 16" White squares. Cut twice diagonally to yield 20 edge triangles. You will use 18 of these.

2. For small quilt, cut two 8½" White squares. For large quilt, cut two 10½" White squares. Cut in half to yield 4 corner triangles.

Note: In the quilt shown on page 27, these corner triangles were not used.

Quilt Assembly

1. Arrange blocks and triangles as shown in the quilt plan on page 43.

2. Stitch together into rows; sew rows together.

3. Add batting and backing. Quilt as desired. Bind edges. See Quilt Finishing, page 72.

BEAR'S PAW

		Strip Width	**No. of Strips**	**Crosscut into:**
Photo	Page 22			
Skill Level	Intermediate			
Border Style	Multiple Squares			
Finished Block Size	10"			
Quilt Size	42" x 42"			

Photo Page 22
Skill Level Intermediate
Border Style Multiple Squares
Finished Block Size 10"
Quilt Size 42" x 42"

Materials: 44"-wide fabric

■ **Navy**	½ yd.
■ **Red**	¾ yd.
■ **Blue**	½ yd.
□ **Beige**	1 yd.
▨ **Light**	1¼ yds.

Batting, backing, binding and thread to finish

Cutting

To simplify the construction of this quilt, first cut the strips listed and crosscut into the squares and rectangles indicated below. Cut the larger pieces from the strips first; then cut the smaller pieces from the remaining strip(s).

	Strip Width	**No. of Strips**	**Crosscut into:**
Navy	4½"	1	4 squares, 4½" x 4½"
	2½"	3	12 squares, 2½" x 2½", from 1 strip; reserve 2 strips
Red	2½"	3	9 squares, 2½" x 2½", from 1 strip; reserve 2 strips
Blue	4½"	1	8 squares, 4½" x 4½"
	2½"	3	16 squares, 2½" x 2½", from 1 strip; reserve 2 strips
Beige	10½"	1	4 rectangles, 8½" x 10½"
	2½"	5	4 rectangles, 2½" x 8½"
			8 rectangles, 2½" x 6½"
			4 rectangles, 2½" x 4½"
			12 squares, 2½" x 2½"
Light	2½"	3	16 rectangles, 2½" x 4½"
			12 squares, 2½" x 2½"

Design Blocks

1. Using the Red and Light fabrics and a 2" finished grid size, construct 1 full grid, following the directions for half-square triangles on page 12. Cut and press.

 Make 16.

2. Sew a 4½" square of Blue to 2 corners of each of the large Beige rectangles as shown, following directions for folded corners on page 11.

 Make 4.

3. Sew pairs of the half-square triangle units together, connecting them with a 2½" square of Beige fabric in the center, as shown. Make 4 units.

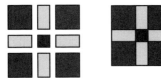
Make 4.

Stitch each unit to 1 of the rectangles from step 2, above.

Make 4.

5. Using the cut squares and rectangles, assemble 1 block as shown.

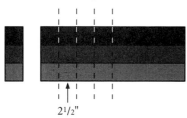
Make 1.

Border Blocks

1. Construct 2 strip sets using reserved 2½"-wide strips of Red, Navy, and Blue as shown. Crosscut into 32 segments, cutting at 2½" intervals.

2½"

2. Make 4 Navy/Red paired-square units as shown, using 2½" squares.

3. Using the strip segments (step 1), paired squares (step 2), and remaining cut squares and rectangles of Beige and Light, assemble the border blocks.

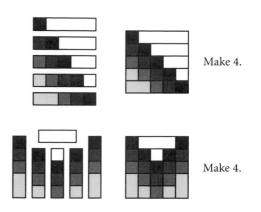
Make 4.

Make 4.

Edge and Corner Triangles

1. Cut two 18" squares from Light fabric. Cut twice diagonally to yield 8 edge triangles.

2. Make 8 Navy/Blue paired-square units as shown, using 2½" squares.

3. From each edge triangle, cut 2 strips, each 2½" wide.

Sew a pair of squares to the straight end of each of 8 strips.
Sew a Blue 2½" square to the straight end of each of the remaining 8 strips.

for each cut on this block add 1" to the triangle –

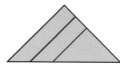

Reassemble the edge triangles and trim as shown.

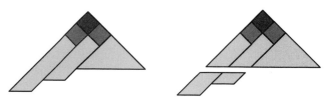

4. Cut two 10" squares of Light fabric. Cut once diagonally to yield 4 corner triangles.

Quilt Assembly

1. Arrange blocks and triangles as shown in the quilt plan on page 46.
2. Stitch together into rows; sew rows together.
3. Add batting and backing. Quilt as desired. Bind edges. See Quilt Finishing, page 72.

ECCENTRIC STARS

Twin Size

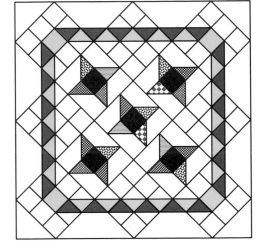

Wall Hanging Size

		Wall Hanging	**Twin Quilt**
Photo	Page 22		
Skill Level	Easy to intermediate		
Border Style	Triangles		
Finished Block Size	7½"		
Quilt Size	Wall Quilt: 31½" x 31½"		
	Twin Quilt: 63" x 95"		

Materials: 44"-wide fabric

		Wall Hanging	**Twin Quilt**
■	**Dark #1**	¾ yd.	1¼ yds.
■	**Dark #2**	¾ yd.	1¾ yds.
☐	**Light**	1⅞ yds.	5¼ yds.

Note: This design is also very effective when done as a scrap quilt. Follow the directions below for the quilt construction, substituting the following units made from your scrap stockpile:

	Wall Hanging	Twin Quilt
Half-Square Triangle Units		
(2 ½" finished)	52	272
Light Squares (3" cut)	28	206
Dark Squares (3" cut)	21	90
Light Rectangles (3" x 8")	4	4
Light Squares (5½" x 5½")	4	18

In addition, you will need two 13" Light squares for the wall hanging or 6 for the twin-size quilt. Cut twice diagonally for 16 edge triangles for wall hanging or 24 edge triangles for twin-size quilt.

For corner triangles, you will need two 8" Light squares. Cut once diagonally for 4 corner triangles.

Design Blocks

1. Using Light and Dark #2 and a 2½" finished grid size, construct 9 full grids for twin size. Construct 1 full grid and 1 half grid for wall size, following the directions for half-square triangles on page 12. Cut and press. Using Dark #1 and Light, construct 2 full grids for twin size and 1 full grid for wall size. Cut and press.

Dark #2/Light	Dark #1
Wall Quilt Make 36.	Wall Quilt Make 16.
Twin Quilt Make 228.	Twin Quilt Make 44.

2. Cut the following 3"-wide strips and crosscut into the number of 3" squares indicated:

	Color	No. of Strips	No. of Squares
Wall Hanging	Dark #1	1	13
	Dark #2	1	8
	Light	4	42
Twin Quilt	Dark #1	6	68
	Dark #2	2	26
	Light	16	206

3. Using the half-square triangles and the 3" squares, assemble star blocks as shown. Reserve remaining units for border and corner blocks.

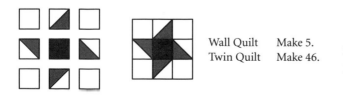

Wall Quilt	Make 5.
Twin Quilt	Make 46.

Border Blocks and Corner Blocks

1. From Light fabric, cut the following strips and crosscut into the squares and rectangles indicated:

	Strip Width	No. of Strips	Crosscut into:
Wall Hanging	3"	1	4 rectangles, 3"x 8"
	5½"	1	4 squares, 5½" x 5½"
Twin Quilt	3"	1	4 rectangles, 3" x 8"
	5½"	4	18 squares, 5½" x 5½"

2. Sew a 3" square of Dark #1 to each Light 5½" square, following the directions for folded corners on page 11.

3. Assemble the border and corner blocks as shown below, using the half-square triangle units reserved earlier.

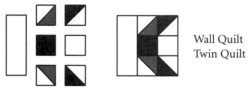

Wall Quilt	Make 4.
Twin Quilt	Make 18.

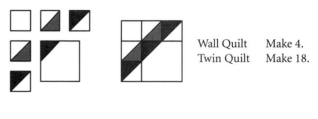

Wall Quilt	Make 4.
Twin Quilt	Make 4.

Edge and Corner Triangles

1. From Light fabric, cut two 13" squares for the wall hanging or six 13" squares for the twin quilt. Cut twice diagonally to yield 8 edge triangles for the wall hanging or 24 edge triangles for the twin quilt. You will use 22 for the twin quilt.

2. Sew one 3" square of Dark #2 to the tips of each edge triangle, following the directions for folded corners on page 11. Make 8 for the wall hanging or 22 for the twin quilt.

3. From Light fabric, cut two 8" squares and cut once diagonally to yield 4 corner triangles.

Quilt Assembly

1. Arrange blocks and triangles as shown in the quilt plan on page 48.
2. Stitch blocks together into rows; sew rows together.
3. Add batting and backing. Quilt as desired. Bind edges. See Quilt Finishing, page 72.

OHIO STAR

Photo	Page 23	
Skill Level	Intermediate	
Border Style	Triangles	
Finished Block Size	7½"	
Quilt Size	42" x 52½"	

Materials: 44"-wide fabric

■ **Dark**	1¼ yds.	
	(or the equivalent in scraps)	
□ **Light**	3¼ yds.	

Star Blocks

1. To make 24 quarter-square triangle units:
a. Construct 1 full grid using Dark and Light fabrics and a grid size for 2½", finished, quarter-square triangles. Follow directions for half- and quarter-square triangles on pages 12–13.
b. Use the resulting half-square triangles to construct the quarter-square triangle units.

Make 24.

2. Cut the following 3"-wide strips and crosscut into squares as indicated:

	No. of Strips	No. of 3" Squares
Dark	1	6
Light	2	24

3. Using quarter-square triangle units and Light and Dark squares, construct the Ohio Star blocks as shown. Make 6 blocks.

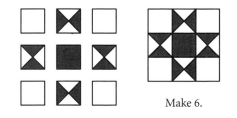

Make 6.

Alternating Blocks

1. Cut the following strips and crosscut into the squares indicated:

	Strip Width	No. of Strips	Crosscut into:
Light	8"	3	12 squares, 8" x 8"
Dark	3"	3	34 squares, 3" x 3"

2. Using the Dark and Light squares and following the directions for folded corners on page 11, make the blocks shown below.

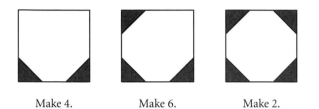

Make 4.   Make 6.   Make 2.

Border Blocks

1. Using the Dark and Light fabrics and a finished grid size of 2½", construct 2 full grids, following the directions for half-square triangle units on page 12. Cut and press.

 Make 38.

2. Cut the following 3"-wide strips and crosscut into squares and rectangles indicated:

	No. of strips	Crosscut into:
Dark	1	4 squares, 3" x 3"
Light	7	20 rectangles, 3" x 5½"
		4 rectangles, 3" x 8"
		32 squares, 3" x 3"

3. Assemble the three different blocks shown below, using the half-square triangle units, squares and rectangles.

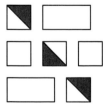

Border Block
Make 10.

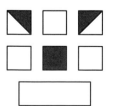

Corner Block A
Make 2.

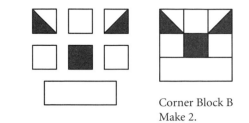

Corner Block B
Make 2.

Edge and Corner Triangles

1. From Light fabric, cut four 13" squares. Cut twice diagonally to yield 16 edge triangles. You will use 14 of these.

2. From Light fabric, cut two 8" squares. Cut once diagonally to yield 4 corner triangles.

Quilt Assembly

1. Arrange blocks and triangles as shown in the quilt plan on page 50.

2. Stitch together into rows; sew rows together.

3. Add batting and backing. Quilt as desired. Bind edges. See Quilt Finishing, page 72.

SEE SAW

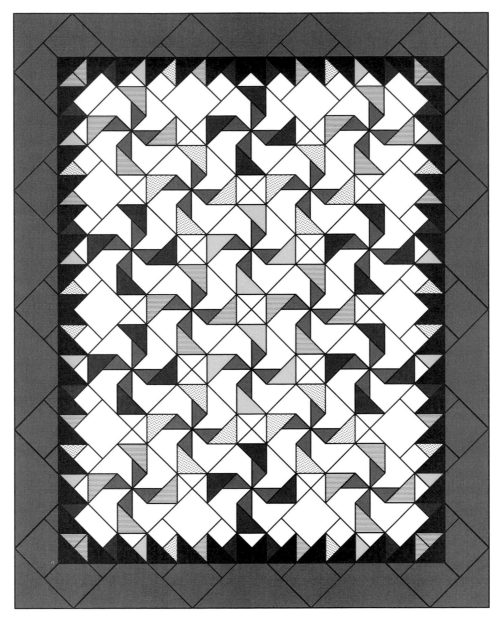

Photo	Page 24	
Skill Level	Intermediate	
Border Style	Shaded Triangles	
Finished Block Size	10"	
Quilt Size	56" x 70"	

Materials: 44"-wide fabric

Large Print	3¼ yds.	
Black	1½ yds.	
White	3½ yds.	
Dark Gold	¾ yd.	
Dark Blue	¾ yd.	
Dark Red	¾ yd.	
Dark Green	¾ yd.	

The Gold, Blue, Red, and Green fabrics are identified as Coordinating Darks in the following directions. Refer to the quilt photo on page 24.

See Saw Blocks

1. Using the Large Print and White fabrics, make 3 full grids, following the directions for half-square triangles on page 12. Use a 2½" finished grid size. Cut and press.

2. Pairing each of the Coordinating Darks with White, construct the following full grids for half-square triangles. Use a grid size of 2½", finished, to make the required number of half-square triangle units.

	No. of Grids	No. of Units
Gold/White	1	16
Blue/White	2	48
Red/White	2	48
Green/White	2	32

3. Cut six 3"-wide strips from White fabric. Cut 72 squares, 3" x 3", from the strips.

4. Assemble blocks as shown, making the required number of each color.

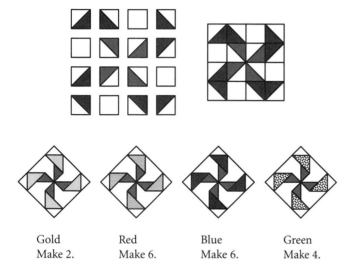

Gold	Red	Blue	Green
Make 2.	Make 6.	Make 6.	Make 4.

Border Blocks

1. Using the Large Print and Black fabrics and a 2½" finished grid size, construct 2 full grids. Follow the directions for half-square triangles on page 12. Cut and press.

2. Pairing each of the Coordinating Darks with Black, construct the following grids for half-square triangles to make the required number of half-square triangle units. Use a 2½" finished grid size.

	No. of Grids	No. of Units
Gold/Black	½	12
Blue/Black	1	16
Red/Black	1	16
Green/Black	½	12

3. Cut the following strips from White and crosscut into the squares and rectangles indicated:

Strip Width	No. of Strips	Crosscut into:
3"	2	20 squares, 3" x 3"
5½"	2	10 squares, 5½" x 5½"
		4 rectangles, 3" x 5½"

4. From Large Print, cut 3 strips, 5½" wide. From them, cut 18 squares, 5½" x 5½".

5. From Black, cut 2 strips, 3" wide. From them, cut 18 squares, 3" x 3".

6. Stitch one 3" Black square to each 5½" square of Large Print, following the directions for folded corners on page 11.

Make 28.

7. Assemble the four different blocks shown below, using the half-square triangles, squares and rectangles.

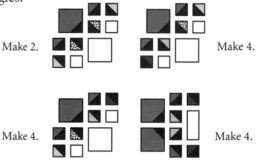

Make 2.   Make 4.

Make 4.   Make 4.

Edge and Corner Triangles

1. From Large Print, cut four 17" squares. Cut twice diagonally to yield 16 edge triangles. You will use 14 of them.

2. From Black, cut 2 strips, 3" wide. Crosscut 14 squares, 3" x 3".

3. Stitch one small Black square to the tip of 14 edge triangles, following the directions for folded corners on page 11.

4. From Large Print, cut two 11" squares. Cut once diagonally to yield 4 corner triangles.

Quilt Assembly

1. Arrange blocks and triangles as shown in the quilt plan on page 52.

2. Stitch together into rows; sew rows together.

3. Add batting and backing. Quilt as desired. Bind edges. See Quilt Finishing, page 72.

GARDEN BASKET

Photo	Page 28
Skill Level	Intermediate
Border Style	Shaded Triangles
Finished Block Size	7½"
Quilt Size	32" x 32"

Materials: 44"-wide fabric
Note: Colors refer to the color photo of "Spring Garden Basket" on page 28.

■	**Dark Green**	¼ yd.
▨	**Rose**	¼ yd.
▩	**Purple**	¼ yd.
□	**Ecru**	¾ yd.
▨	**Pink**	½ yd.
■	**Light Green**	½ yd.
▨	**Large Print**	1 yd.

Batting, backing, binding and thread to finish

Basket Blocks and Border Squares

1. Cut and construct the required number of half-square triangle units, following the directions on page 12. Since this quilt requires only a small number of half-square triangle units of each fabric combination, you do not need to construct full grids, only the required number of grid squares indicated below.

	No. of Grid Squares	No. of Half-Square Triangle Units
Dark Green/Ecru	2	4
Rose/Ecru	2	3
Purple/Ecru	4	7
Pink/Light Green	8	16
Light Green/ Large Print	8	16

2. Cut the following strips from the fabrics indicated and crosscut into squares and rectangles as directed:

	Strip Width	No. of Strips	Crosscut into:
Ecru	5½"	1	4 rectangles, 5½"x 8"
	3"	2	10 squares, 3" x 3"
			5 rectangles, 3" x 5½"
Pink	3"	1	4 squares 3" x 3"
Light Green	3"	1	12 squares, 3" x 3"
Large Print	3"	2	4 squares, 3" x 3"
			4 rectangles, 3" x 8"

3. From Dark Green, cut 1 square, 5½" x 5½", for basket base. Sew a 3" square of Ecru to one corner of the basket base square, following the directions for folded corners on page 11.

4. Make the following blocks using the half-square triangle units and the cut squares and rectangles.

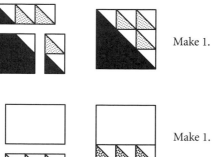

Make 1.

Make 1.

Make 1.

Make 1.

Make 1.

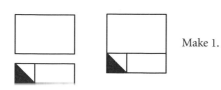

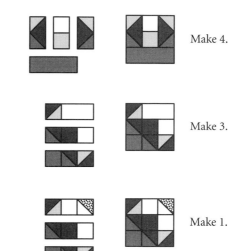

Make 4.

Make 3.

Make 1.

Edge and Corner Triangles

1. From Large Print, cut two 13" squares and cut twice diagonally to yield 8 edge triangles.
2. Sew a 3" square of Light Green to the tip of each edge triangle, following the directions for folded corners on page 11.

3. From Large Print, cut two 8" squares and cut once diagonally to yield 4 corner triangles.

Quilt Assembly

1. Arrange blocks and triangles as shown in the diagram below.

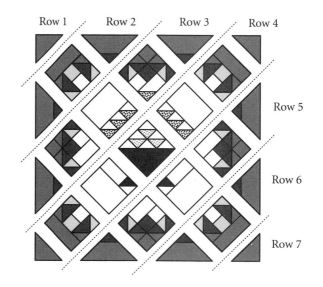

Row 1   Row 2   Row 3   Row 4   Row 5   Row 6   Row 7

2. Stitch together into rows; sew rows together.
3. Add batting and backing. Quilt as desired. Bind edges. See Quilt Finishing, page 72.

CELEBRATION

Photo	Page 21
Skill Level	Advanced
Border Style	Triangles
Finished Block Size	12"
Quilt Size	51" x 51"

Materials: 44"-wide fabric

▨	**Blue**	¼ yd. each of 9 fabrics
■	**Dark**	¾ yd.
☐	**White**	3 yds.
■	**Red**	Scrap (optional for center star)

Star Blocks

1. Make templates on page 70 for all star pattern pieces. Cut from Blue fabrics as indicated on templates. If desired, cut 4 of Template 6 from Red scrap for the center star only, as shown in the quilt photo on page 21.

Note: To make cutting easier, divide star fabrics into Groups A and B. Use pieces cut from Group A in the vertical and horizontal points of each star block. Use pieces from Group B in remaining (diagonal) points.

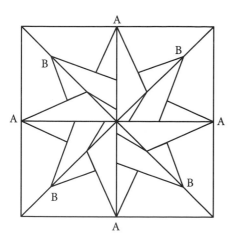

2. Assemble 5 star blocks, following the piecing diagram below.

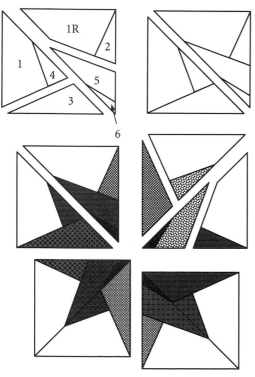

Make 5.

Border Blocks

1. Using the Dark and White fabrics and a 3" finished grid size, construct 1 full grid and 1 half grid, following the directions for half-square triangles on page 12. Assemble 8 pinwheel units.

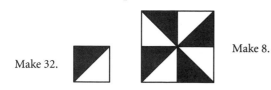

Make 32.   Make 8.

2. Cut the following strips and crosscut into the rectangles indicated:

	Strip Width	No. of Strips	Crosscut into:
Dark	2"	2	Reserve for step 3, below.
White	2"	2	Reserve for step 3, below.
	3½"	7	4 rectangles, 3½" x 12½"
			8 rectangles, 3½" x 9½"
			20 rectangles, 3½" x 6½"

3. Sew the 2"-wide strips of Dark and White into 2 strip sets as shown. Crosscut strip sets into 2"-wide segments. Sew segments together to make 16 checkerboard squares.

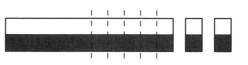

4. Assemble blocks, following piecing diagrams below.

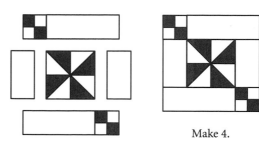

Make 4.

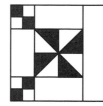

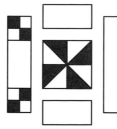

Make 4.

Edge and Corner Triangles

1. Cut two 19" squares of White. Cut twice diagonally to yield a total of 8 edge triangles.
2. Cut two 12" squares of White. Cut once diagonally to yield 4 corner triangles.

Quilt Assembly

1. Arrange all blocks and triangles as shown in the quilt plan on page 56.
2. Stitch blocks together into rows; sew rows together.
3. Add batting and backing. Quilt as desired. Bind edges. See Quilt Finishing, page 72.

QUILTMAKER'S DREAMS

Photo	Page 29
Skill Level	Advanced
Border Style	Triangles
Finished Block Size	12"
Quilt Size	50" x 66"

Materials: 44"-wide fabric

☐	**Light Print**	3¾ yds.
■	**Dark Navy**	1 yd.
■	**Navy Print**	1 yd.
▦	**Rose**	⅜ yd.
▨	**Blue Stripe**	1¼ yds.
☐	**Gray Print**	½ yd.

Star Blocks

1. Cut pieces for the Piecemaker's Block, using the templates on page 71. Assemble Unit 1 and Unit 2 following the piecing diagram below. Make 32 of each unit.

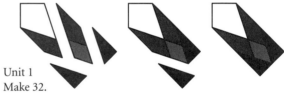

Unit 1
Make 32.

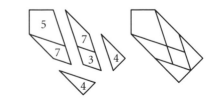

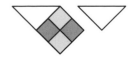

Unit 2
Make 32.

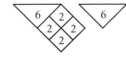

2. Assemble Unit 1 and Unit 2 with Template #1 to complete block as shown. Make 8 blocks.

Make 8.

Border Blocks

1. Construct the following grids, referring to the directions for half-square triangles on page 12 and using the fabric combinations listed. Cut and press.

Make 20.   Make 80.   Make 40.

	Finished Grid Size	No. of Grids
Light Print/Blue Stripe	4"	1
Light Print/Dark Navy	2"	3½
Light Print/Navy Print	2"	2

2. Using the small half-square triangle units, make 20 Light Print/Dark Navy pinwheel squares and 10 Light Print/Navy Print pinwheel squares.

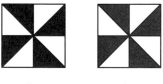

Make 10.   Make 20.

3. From Light Print, cut 5 strips, 4½" wide. Crosscut into 36 squares, 4½" x 4½".

4. From Light Print, cut 1 square, 5¼" x 5¼" and 2 squares, 4⅞" x 4⅞". From Blue Stripe, cut 1 square, 5¼" x 5¼". Place the 5¼" squares of Light Print and Blue Stripe right sides together and draw a diagonal line through the center, crossing the seamline. Stitch ¼" away on both sides of the line, cut apart and press.

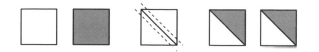

5. Place each resulting half-square triangle right sides together with one of the 4⅞" squares of Light Print. Draw a diagonal line through the square, crossing the seam line. Stitch ¼" away on both sides of the line, cut apart and press. You should have 4 quarter-square triangle units.

5. Assemble the two different border blocks as shown.

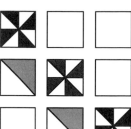 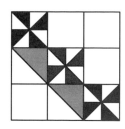

Make 6.

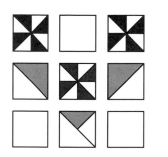 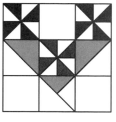

Make 4.

Edge and Corner Triangles

1. From Light Print, cut three 19" squares. Cut twice diagonally to yield 12 edge triangles. You will use 10 of these.

2. From Blue Stripe, cut 2 strips, 4½" wide, and cross-cut 10 squares, 4½" x 4½".

3. Stitch a 4½" square of blue stripe to the tips of 10 edge triangles, following the directions for folded corners on page 11.

I-150

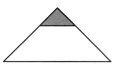

4. From Light Print, cut two 12" squares. Cut once diagonally to yield 4 corner triangles.

Quilt Assembly

1. Arrange blocks and triangles as shown in the quilt plan on page 58.

2. Stitch together into rows; sew rows together.

3. Add batting and backing. Quilt as desired. Bind edges. See Quilt Finishing, page 72.

SNOW CRYSTALS

Photo	Page 30
Skill Level	Intermediate
Border Style	Pleated Ribbon
Finished Block Size	8"
Quilt Size	34" x 34"

Materials: 44"-wide fabric

▦	Gray	½ yd.
☐	White	½ yd.
■	Dark Teal	½ yd.
▨	Medium Teal	½ yd.
■	Pink	¼ yd.
■	Black	¼ yd.
▨	Print	1¼ yds.

Design Blocks

1. Using the fabric combinations listed and a 2" finished grid size, construct the following grids, or portions of grids. Follow the directions for half-square triangles on page 12. Cut and press.

	No. of grids	No. of Half-Square Triangles
White/Print	1½	32
Pink/Black	½	12
White/Black	2 grid squares	4
White/Pink	2 grid squares	4
Gray/Black	4 grid squares	8
Gray/Pink	4 grid squares	8

2. Cut the following strips and crosscut into the squares and rectangles indicated:

	Strip Width	No. of Strips	Crosscut into:
White	2½"	1	12 squares, 2½" x 2½"
Gray	4½"	1	4 rectangles, 4½"x 8½"
Print	4½"	1	1 square, 4½" x 4½"

3. Sew a 2½" White square to 2 corners of each Gray rectangle as shown, following the directions for folded corners on page 11.

4. Using the half-square triangle units and rectangles prepared in step 3, assemble 1 center star block and the 4 surrounding blocks as shown. Reserve all remaining half-square triangle units for the border blocks and edge triangles.

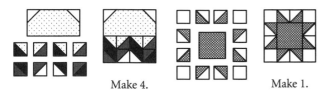

Make 4. Make 1.

Border Blocks

1. Using the fabric combinations listed and a 2" finished grid size, construct the following grids, or portions of grids. Follow the directions for half-square triangles on page 12. Cut and press. Reserve extra units of Dark Teal/Medium Teal for the edge triangles.

	No. of grids	No. of Half-Square Triangles
Dark Teal/Medium Teal	3	60
Gray/White	1	20
White/Dark Teal	2 grid squares	4
White/Medium Teal	2 grid squares	4
White/Print	1	24

2. From Print, cut 1 strip, 2½" wide. Crosscut 12 squares, 2½" x 2½".

3. From Gray, cut 1 strip, 2½" wide. Crosscut 8 squares, 2½" x 2½".

4. Assemble the border blocks as shown.

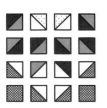

Make 4.

Make 4.

Edge Triangles and Corner Triangles

1. From Print, cut two 16" squares. Cut twice diagonally to yield 8 edge triangles.

2. Cut 1 strip, 2½" wide, from one side of each edge triangle.

3. From White, cut 1 strip, 2½" wide. Crosscut 16 squares, 2½" x 2½". Sew 1 square to the straight end of each edge-triangle strip and 1 square to the tip of each edge triangle, following the directions for folded corners on page 11. Make sure the folded corners are stitched in the correct direction, comparing them to the diagram below.

Reassemble the edge triangles, using the half-square triangles reserved earlier. Make 8.

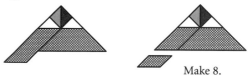

Make 8.

4. From Print, cut two 8½" squares. Cut once diagonally to yield 4 corner triangles.

Quilt Assembly

1. Arrange blocks and triangles as shown below.

2. Stitch together into rows; sew rows together.

3. Add batting and backing. Quilt as desired. Bind edges. See Quilt Finishing, page 72.

CONFETTI MEDALLION

Photo	Page 26
Skill Level	Advanced
Border Style	Multiple Borders
Finished Block Size	10"
Quilt Size	98" x 112"

Materials: 44"-wide fabric

	Light #1	6 yds.
	Light #2	2¾ yds.
	Light Paisley	1¾ yds.
*	**Blue #1**	1¼ yds.
	Blue # 2	1¼ yds.
	Blue #3	¾ yd.
	Blue #4	¾ yd.
**	**Red #1**	1¼ yds.
	Red #2	1¼ yds.
	Red #3	1¼ yds.
	Red #4	1¼ yds.
	Teal	1 yd.
	Dark Paisley	4⅜ yds.

* If you prefer to use one Blue throughout the quilt, you will need a total of 4 yards.

** If you prefer to use one Red throughout the quilt, you will need a total of 5 yards.

Star and Pinwheel Blocks

1. Cut the following strips and crosscut into the squares and rectangles indicated:

	Strip Width	No. of Strips	Crosscut into:
Light #1	5½"	5	60 rectangles, 3" x 5½"
	10½"	1	12 rectangles, 3" x 10½"
Blues	3"	4	48 squares, 3" x 3"
		(1 of each)	(12 squares from each strip)
Reds	3"	4	48 squares, 3" x 3"
		(1 of each)	(12 squares from each strip)
Lt. Paisley	3"	4	48 squares, 3" x 3"
Teal	3"	2	24 squares, 3" x 3"

2. From each of the following fabric combinations, construct 1 half grid, using a 2½" finished grid size and following the directions for half-square triangles on page 12. Cut and press. You should have 12 half-square triangle units of each combination.
    Red #1/Blue #1
    Red #2/Blue #2
    Red #3/Blue #3
    Red #4/Blue #4

3. Using the Red/Blue half-square triangle units, make pinwheels for the center of the star blocks. Alternate the red and blue triangles as shown.

4. Sew 1 Red and 1 Blue 3" square to the ends of 48 Light #1 rectangles (3" x 5½"), following the directions for folded corners on page 11. Make sure the red and blue fabrics are all in the position shown below.

Add squares of Light Paisley to each end of 24 of the rectangles with folded corners.

5. Assemble star blocks as shown. Make 12.

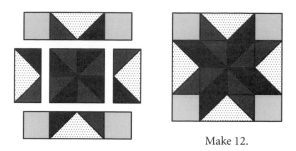

Make 12.

6. Construct 1 full grid of half-square triangles, using Light #1 and Dark Paisley and a 2½" finished grid size. Follow the directions for half-square triangles on page 12. Cut and press. Make 6 pinwheels.

7. Sew a 3" Teal square to each end of the 3" x 10½" rectangles of Light #1, following the directions for folded corners on page 11.

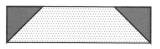

8. Arrange the pinwheels and rectangles with folded corners and 3" x 5½" rectangles of Light #1 to form the Pinwheel blocks as shown. Make 6.

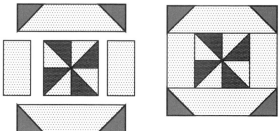

Make 6.

Plain Squares

1. Cut the following strips and crosscut into squares as indicated:

	Strip Width	No. of Strips	Crosscut into:
Light #2	10½"	5	14 squares, 10½" x 10½"
Teal	3"	3	38 squares, 3" x 3"
Blue #1	3"	2	18 squares, 3" x 3"

2. Following directions for folded corners on page 11, make the following units.

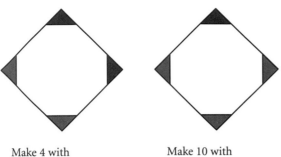

Make 4 with
2 Blue #1 corners and
2 Teal corners.

Make 10 with
1 Blue #1 corner and
3 Teal corners.

Border Blocks

In each of the three pieced borders, there are two different blocks. One is used for all four sides of the border and the other to turn the corner gracefully.

Inner Border

1. Cut the following strips and crosscut into squares as indicated:

	Strip Width	No. of Strips	Crosscut into:
Light #1	5½"	4	22 squares, 5½" x 5½"
Light #2	5½"	2	14 squares, 5½" x 5½"
Light Paisley	3"	6	72 squares, 3" x 3"
Blue #1	3"	2	22 squares, 3" x 3"
Blue #2	3"	2	14 squares, 3" x 3"

2. From each of the following color combinations, construct 1 full grid for half-square triangles, using a 2½" finished grid size and following the directions for half-square triangles on page 12. Cut and press. You should have 24 half-square triangle units of each combination.

   Light #1/Blue #3
Light #2/Blue #3
Light #1/Blue #4
Light#2/Blue #4

3. Sew a 3" square of Blue #2 to each 5½" square of Light #1, following the directions for folded corners on page 11. Do the same with 3" squares of Blue #1 and 5½" squares of Light #2.

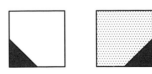

4. Assemble the inner border blocks as shown, making sure identical blues are not opposite each other in the blocks.

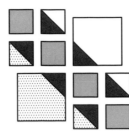
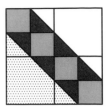

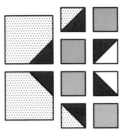
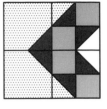

Make 14.

Make 4.

Middle Border

1. Cut the following strips and crosscut into the squares and rectangles indicated:

	Strip Width	No. of Strips	Crosscut into:
Light #1	5½"	4	44 rectangles, 3" x 5½"
	8"	4	44 rectangles, 3" x 8"
Blue #2	3"	2	18 squares, 3" x 3"
Red #1	3"	2	26 squares, 3" x 3"
Teal	3"	4	44 squares, 3" x 3"

2. From each of the following color combinations, construct a half grid, using a 2½" finished grid size and following the directions for half-square triangles on page 12. Cut and press. You should have 12 half-square triangle units of each combination.

Light #1/Blue #1   Light #1/Red #1
Light #1/Blue #2   Light #1/Red #2
Light #1/Blue #3   Light #1/Red #3
Light #1/Blue #4   Light #1/Red #4

3. Sew a 3" square of Blue #2 to one end of each of 18 rectangles (3" x 8") of Light #1, following the directions for folded corners on page 11. Sew a 3" square of Red #2 to one end of each 26 Light #1 rectangles.

Make 18.   Make 26.

4. Assemble Pinwheels, pairing 2 reds and 2 blues to make one set of 11 blocks and the remaining reds and blues for a second set of 11 blocks.

5. Assemble Pinwheel blocks as shown, making 2 corner blocks to match each set of pinwheels.

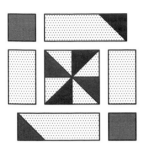 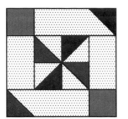

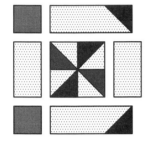 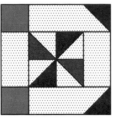

Make 18.

Make 4.

Outer Border

1. Cut the following strips and crosscut into the squares indicated:

	Strip Width	No. of Strips	Crosscut into:
Light #1	5½"	4	22 squares, 5½" x 5½"
Dark Paisley	5½"	5	30 squares, 5½" x 5½"
Light Paisley	3"	8	104 squares, 3" x 3"
Red #1	3"	3	30 squares, 3" x 3"
Red #2	3"	2	22 squares, 3" x 3"

2. Using the fabric combinations listed and a 2½" finished grid size, construct the following grids. Refer to the directions for half-square triangles on page 12. Cut and press.

	No. of Grids
Light #1/Red #3	1
Light #1/Red #4	1½
Dark Paisley/Red #3	1½
Dark Paisley/Red #4	1

3. Sew a 3" square of Red #2 to each Light #1 square and a 3" square of Red #1 to a Dark Paisley square, following directions for folded corners on page 11.

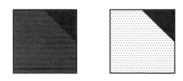

4. Assemble blocks as shown, making sure that identical reds do not end up opposite each other in the finished blocks.

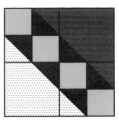 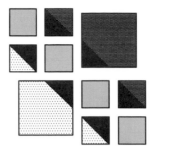

Make 22.

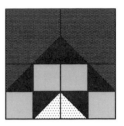 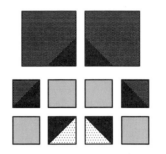

Make 4.

Edge and Corner Triangles

1. From Dark Paisley, cut seven 17" squares. Cut twice diagonally to yield 28 edge triangles. You will use only 26.

2. From Red #2, cut 2 strips, 3" wide. Crosscut 26 squares, 3" x 3".

3. Sew a square of Red #2 to the tip of each of 26 edge triangles.

Make 26.

4. From Dark Paisley, cut two 11" squares. Cut once diagonally to yield 4 corner triangles.

Quilt Assembly

1. Arrange blocks and triangles as shown in the quilt plan on page 62.

2. Stitch together into rows; sew rows together.

3. Add batting and backing. Quilt as desired. Bind edges. See Quilt Finishing, page 72.

APPLIQUÉ QUILT

Photo	Page 30
Skill Level	Intermediate
Border Style	Pleated Ribbon
Finished Block Size	10"
Quilt Size	42" x 42"

Materials: 44"-wide fabric

☐	**White**	1¾ yds.
■	**Green #1**	¾ yd.
■	**Green #2**	¾ yd.
▨	**Pink**	¼ yd.
▨	**Red print**	¼ yd.
▨	**Red/Green Print**	1¾ yds.

Note: Above fabric requirements include an extra ¼ yd. for appliqué pieces.

Batting, backing, binding and thread to finish

Appliqué Blocks

1. From White, cut 5 background squares, 10½" x 10½".

2. Cut and appliqué the designs to each of the White background squares using the appliqué templates on page 69. You may make the 5 blocks as shown in the quilt on page 30 or design your own appliqué blocks using the 8 templates provided.

    Use your favorite hand or machine appliqué method. Use bias bars or another favorite method to make the ³⁄₁₆"-wide (finished) bias stems.

Bluebirds and Tulips

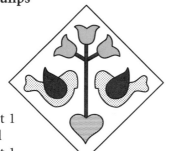

Template #2: Cut 1
   and 1 reversed
Template #4: Cut 1
Template #5: Cut 3
Template #8: Cut 1 and 1 reversed
16"-long strip for ³⁄₁₆" (finished width) stems

Tulips Go Round

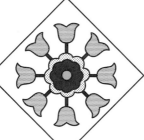

Template #1: Cut 1
Template #3: Cut 1
Template #5: Cut 8
Template #6: Cut 1
16"-long bias strip for ³⁄₁₆" (finished width) stems

Crossed Tulips

Template #3: Cut 1
Template #5: Cut 4
Template #6: Cut 1
Template #7: Cut 4 and 4 reversed
12"-long bias strip for ³⁄₁₆" (finished width) stems

Sarah's Block

Template #4: Cut 1
Template #5: Cut 3
Template #7: Cut 4 and 4 reversed
16"-long strip for ³⁄₁₆" (finished width) stems

Flower Wreath

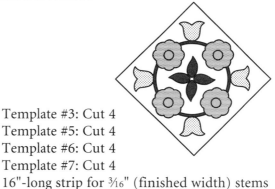

Template #3: Cut 4
Template #5: Cut 4
Template #6: Cut 4
Template #7: Cut 4
16"-long strip for ³⁄₁₆" (finished width) stems

Border Blocks

1. Using the fabric combinations listed and a 2" finished grid size, construct the following grids. Follow the directions for half-square triangles on page 12. Cut and press.

	No. of Grids
White/Red-Green Print	1
Green #1/Green #2	3½*

* Reserve extra units of Green #1/Green #2 for the edge triangles.

2. Cut the following strips and crosscut into squares and rectangles as indicated:

	Strip Width	No. of Strips	Crosscut into:
White	2½"	4	44 squares, 2½" x 2½"
			4 rectangles, 2½" x 6½"
	4½"	1	4 squares, 4½" x 4½"
			8 rectangles, 2½" x 4½"
Green #1	2½"	1	2 squares, 2½" x 2½"
Green #2	2½"	1	2 squares, 2½" x 2½"
Red/ Green Print	4½"	2	12 squares, 4½" x 4½"

3. Sew a White square to each Red/Green Print square following the directions for folded corners on page 11.

Make 4.

4. Cut one 3¼" square from White and one from Red/Green Print. Using these 2 squares, construct two half-square triangle units. Cut and press.

Make 2.

Cut two 2⅞" squares of Red/Green Print. Place each square right sides together with a half-square triangle unit and draw a diagonal line through the center, crossing the seam allowance of the triangle unit. Stitch ¼" away on each side of the line. Cut on the line. You should have 4 squares made of 3 triangles. Use these for the corner blocks.

Make 4.

5. Assemble blocks as shown.

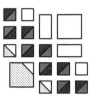

Make 2.

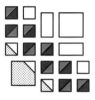

Make 2.

Make 2.

Make 2.

Note: The quilt in the color photo on page 30 has slightly different corners than those shown here, which are much easier to make and more attractive. (If you prefer the ones in the photo, you will need to make 4 additional sets of quarter-square triangles.)

Edge and Corner Triangles

1. From Red/Green Print, cut two 18" squares. Cut twice diagonally to yield 8 edge triangles.
2. Cut 1 strip, 2½" wide, from each edge triangle as shown.

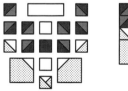

3. Sew a 2½" White square (remaining from previous steps) to the straight end of each strip, following the directions for folded corners on page 11. Make sure stitching line is parallel to the angled end of the strip, referring to diagrams below. Stitch a reserved half-square triangle unit to the straight end of the strip, following the diagrams for the correct placement of dark and light fabrics in each of the blocks. Reassemble edge triangles and trim excess strip even with long edge of triangle.

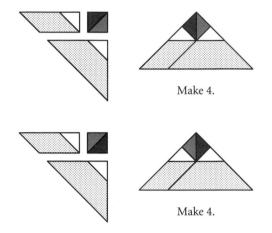

Make 4.

Make 4.

4. From Red/Green Print, cut two 10½" squares. Cut once diagonally to yield 4 corner triangles.

Quilt Assembly

1. Arrange blocks and triangles as shown below.

2. Stitch blocks together into rows; sew the rows together.
3. Add batting and backing. Quilt as desired. Bind edges. See Quilt Finishing, page 72.

APPLIQUÉ TEMPLATES

Appliqué Templates
No seam allowances included.

TEMPLATES

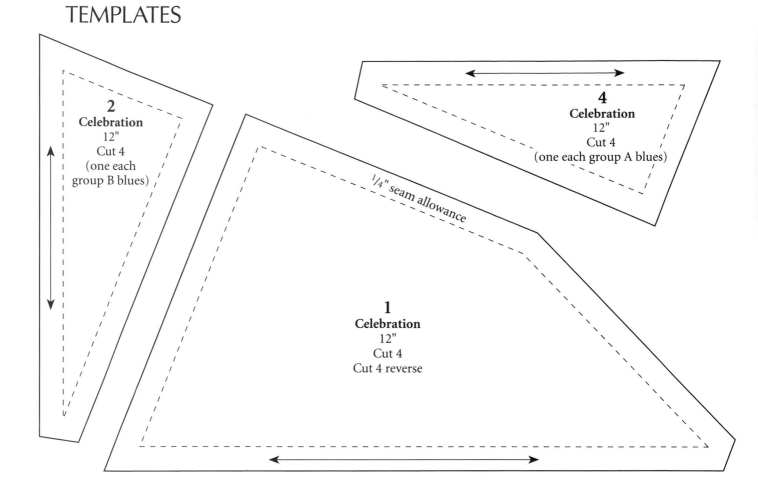

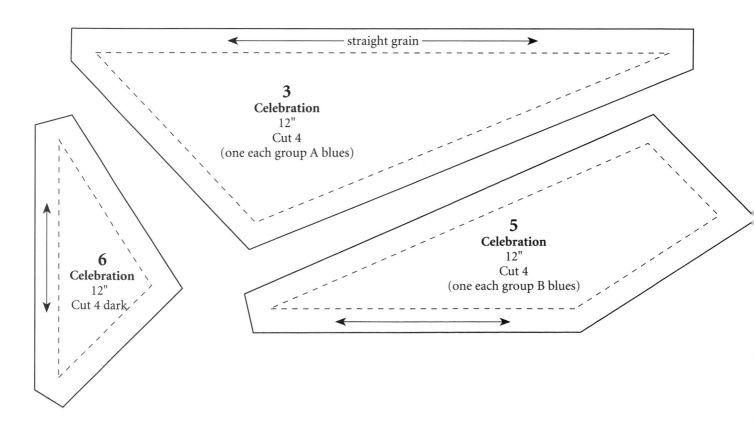

2
Celebration
12"
Cut 4
(one each group B blues)

¼" seam allowance

1
Celebration
12"
Cut 4
Cut 4 reverse

4
Celebration
12"
Cut 4
(one each group A blues)

straight grain

3
Celebration
12"
Cut 4
(one each group A blues)

5
Celebration
12"
Cut 4
(one each group B blues)

6
Celebration
12"
Cut 4 dark

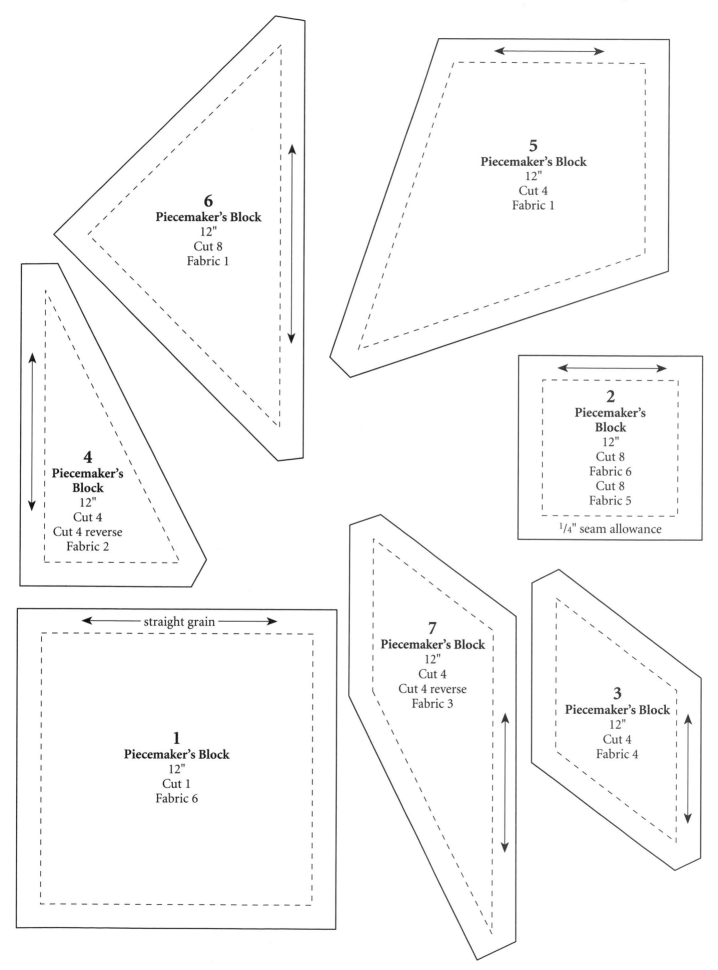

6
Piecemaker's Block
12"
Cut 8
Fabric 1

5
Piecemaker's Block
12"
Cut 4
Fabric 1

4
Piecemaker's Block
12"
Cut 4
Cut 4 reverse
Fabric 2

2
Piecemaker's Block
12"
Cut 8
Fabric 6
Cut 8
Fabric 5

¹/₄" seam allowance

straight grain

1
Piecemaker's Block
12"
Cut 1
Fabric 6

7
Piecemaker's Block
12"
Cut 4
Cut 4 reverse
Fabric 3

3
Piecemaker's Block
12"
Cut 4
Fabric 4

QUILT FINISHING

There are many sources of information about basting and quilting quilts, either by hand or machine. Marsha McCloskey's *Lessons in Machine Piecing*, or Trudie Hughes' *Template-Free™ Quiltmaking* have very good directions for these techniques. I have not included them here because of their wide availability elsewhere.

QUILT BACKS

Although some directions for quilt backings specify that seams should be lengthwise and away from the center of the quilt, I prefer to calculate the yardage required for the backs of my quilts to provide the least amount of excess fabric. (Notice that I do not use the word "waste." All excess fabric from the back of my quilts becomes strips, half-square triangle units, or pieces for the front of other quilts. Nothing is wasted!)

For all quilts up to 84" long, I piece the backing with one crosswise seam in the center. To piece this backing, measure the width of the quilt, add 6", and double this measurement. This is the amount of fabric you will need to purchase in inches. (Divide by 36 to calculate yards.)

Backing for quilts up to 84" long

For quilts that are longer than 84" and up to 84" wide, I piece the backing with one lengthwise seam in the center. To piece this backing, measure the length of the quilt, add 6", and double this measurement. This is the amount of fabric you will need to purchase in inches. (Divide by 36" to calculate yards.)

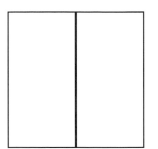

Backing for quilts longer than 84" and up to 84" wide

I piece backings for quilts that need to be even larger than this, using three lengths of fabric. To piece a backing of this size, measure the shortest side, add 6", triple this measurement, and purchase that amount of fabric in inches. (Divide by 36" to calculate yards.)

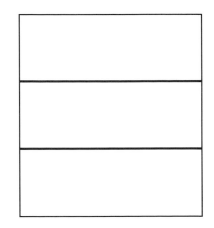

Backing for quilts up to 120" in either length or width

BINDING

When preparing to bind *Painless Border* quilts, I first decide how wide I want the outer border to be. Because of the method used to construct these quilts, the outer border (composed of portions of pieced blocks and edge and corner triangles) is probably a large, multicolored print. You can cut off as much of it as you wish to make the outer border the desired finished width.

After determining how wide you want the border, use a wide acrylic ruler to measure and mark the desired border width between the outermost edge of the pieced border blocks and the raw edge of the quilt. Use the marked line instead of the raw edge of the quilt when positioning binding strips for stitching.

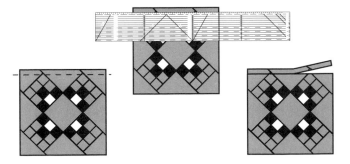

Chosen border size; trim away excess border fabric.

I cut straight-grain binding strips across the full width of the fabric. Strips are cut 2½" wide. The yardage required to cut straight-grain binding for standard-size quilts is listed below. These measurements are very closely calculated and do not allow any extra fabric for mistakes in cutting; you may choose to purchase more than this, planning to add the extra yardage to your scraps!

Quilt Size	Yardage
Crib	⅜ yd.
Lap	½ yd.
Twin	⅝ yd.
Full, Queen	¾ yd.
King	1 yd.

Sew the strips together to make one long strip. Press seam allowances open, then press the strip in half, wrong sides together. Open out the strip at one end and fold the corner to form a 45° angle.

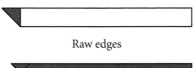

Raw edges

Do not trim away excess backing and batting at the outer edge of the quilt after it has been quilted. Wait until the binding has been attached. Pin the binding strip to the edge of the quilt top with raw edges even, beginning about 6" away from one corner and ending at the next corner. Stitch, using a ⅜" seam allowance and ending ⅜" from the adjacent edge.

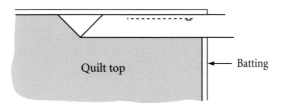

Quilt top — Batting

To miter the corner, fold the binding strip at a 45° angle away from the quilt. Fold the binding strip back on itself, parallel with the next edge of the quilt. Stitch.

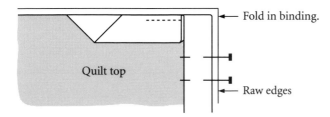

Fold in binding.

Quilt top

Raw edges

Remove the quilt from the sewing machine and refold the miter. Beginning at the raw edge, sew the binding to the next side of the quilt, ending ⅜" from the adjacent edge.

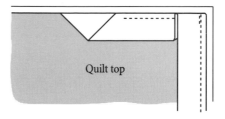

Quilt top

Repeat the above process for each corner.

Where the end of the binding meets the beginning, open out the folded edge and place the end of the binding inside the fold. Refold the binding with the raw end inside.

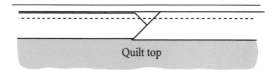

Quilt top

Repeat the above step for each corner. Stitch through all thicknesses where the two ends of the binding meet.

Trim the edge of the quilt back and batting about ⅜" beyond the raw edge of the quilt top. Fold the binding over and handstitch on the wrong side, mitering each corner as shown below.

APPENDIX —BORDER DESIGNS

BIG AND LITTLE SQUARES AND TRIANGLES

Both the Big and Little Squares and Big and Little squares with Triangles borders are shown here with some suggested colorings. The blocks required to make the border are outlined within the diagram of each quilt.

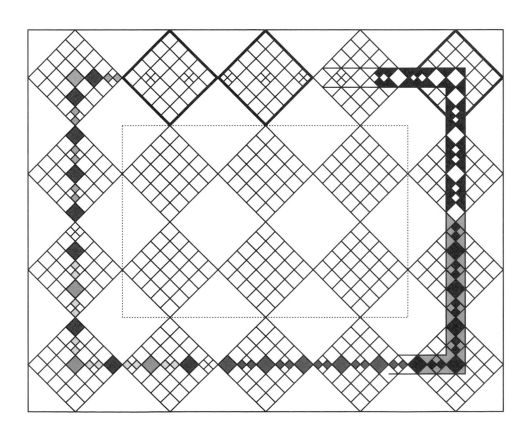

SQUARES AND TRIANGLES

Borders made of squares and triangles can encompass just one square between the triangles or they can enclose multiple squares as shown in the Five-Patch diagram below. If more than one square is enclosed, the edge triangles and inside squares will need to be pieced.

MULTIPLE SQUARES

Borders with multiple squares can be colored in many different ways to produce different effects. The edge triangles and the blocks just inside the border will have to be pieced to maintain the continuity of the design.

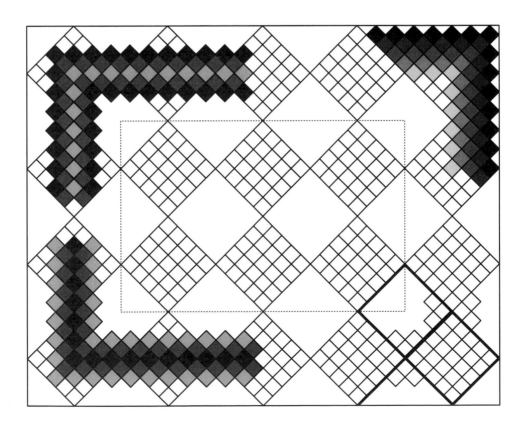

TRIANGLES

Three different configurations are possible with just a row of triangles around the edge of the quilt. Adding a second row of triangles presents even more options.

SHADED TRIANGLES

Several different corner treatments are offered for borders of shaded triangles. Any of them would be attractive on a quilt.

TWISTED RIBBON

When you use a grid with an odd number of squares (Five Patch or Ninepatch) for a twisted ribbon border, you must use an even number of blocks both down and across to make the corner turn properly.

All twisted ribbon borders need blocks in one arrangement for the top and bottom of the quilt and another arrangement for the sides of the quilt. All the required blocks for all grid sizes are outlined with a dark line here.

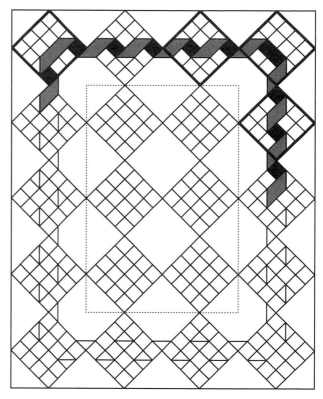

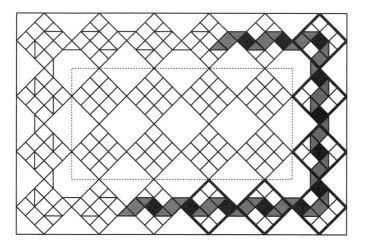

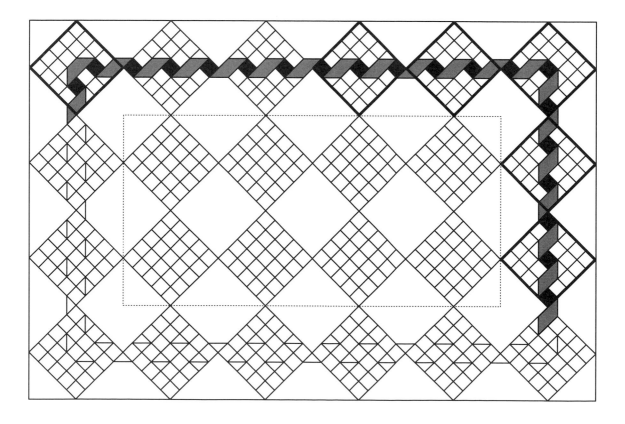

PLEATED RIBBON

Half-square triangles may be used to separate the pieced border from the outer border if necessary. The required blocks are shown above.

Two different corner options are shown in this version of the border. The corners on the top of the quilt are much simpler to construct, using only squares, whereas the corners on the bottom require several different quarter-square triangle units. See this border on the Appliqué quilt, page 30.